A Place in Time

Joy Massey

Cherry Pie Publishing

Copyright © 2019 by Joy Massey.

All rights reserved. No part of this publication may be reproduced, stored in a retrieval system, or transmitted in any form or by any means, electronic, mechanical, photocopying, recording, or otherwise, without the prior written permission of the copyright holder, except brief quotations used in a review.

Some of the names in this narrative have been changed.

Design by Meadowlark Publishing Services.

Flower photo on page 21 © iStockphoto.com/artist: AntiMartina. All other illustrations courtesy of the author.

Published by Cherry Pie Publishing.

Manufactured in the United States of America.
ISBN 978-0-578-58256-6

Published 2019

To all those who follow their hearts

Preface

The Land drew me, called to me in a voice that spoke directly to my soul.

I can hardly believe I'm living here now, on this three-hundred-acre ranch outside of Occidental in northern California. From the top of the hill where I'm standing, I can see a wide expanse of the Pacific Ocean on the horizon. The coastal hills are a patchwork of tall tangled grasses and forests of redwood, fir, oak, and wild lilac.

Here I have no rent to pay. No mortgage payments. I am neither landowner nor tenant. I have no utility bills because I have no electricity and no phone. I have no alarm clock to wake me for work in the morning because I don't have a job. I don't have running water indoors or indoor plumbing, which the Health Department would have you believe is essential, or at least legal. My shelter, which was at first just a tent, does not have studs in the walls eighteen inches apart, one of the many requirements for a legal structure. Yet what seems ascetic to some turns out to be almost incomprehensible luxury—the luxuries of silence, time, autonomy, privacy, simplicity, luxuries now that at one time were taken for granted.

Geographically, the land has everything. Grassy meadows change from green in spring to gold in summer. Edible plants and wild berries grow in abundance. There are springs here, more than on any of the surrounding ridges, pure water bubbling up from rocks or marshes. Rare wildflowers bloom here—baby blue eyes, blue-eyed grass, and mariposa lily. Deer are almost tame on this ridge because hunting has been prohibited for so long. Hawks soar through blue skies and owls hoot at sunset.

I have found myself in a real place where you can live free in the woods. Make your own shelter. Drink from a spring. Lie naked in the sun. Pick wild greens for dinner. Just living here is a powerful statement.

The people here can walk in the dark. They can feel the way with their feet. At first it amazed me, and then I began to learn it too. In this place, I sleep when it gets dark and wake when it gets light. I have begun to feel the moon, unable to sleep when it is full and passing over. I've lost the cycle that was programmed into me with artificial light. I've begun to feel a new rhythm.

Here we grow our own food, set up our own water systems, build our own homes, and raise our children, all without bureaucratic intervention.

I had only dreamed of living in a place like this, and now here I am, and the dream has come true.

1

What we are doing is running a pilot study in survival. Get a piece of land and see who it attracts.
—Lou Gottlieb

It was 1978 and I was twenty-six years old when I found myself standing at the front gate of Wheeler's Ranch. I thought of Lou Gottlieb, who had bought thirty acres north of San Francisco in the early 1960s. He had deeded it to God and called it Morningstar. I had heard some say it was a social experiment, about the land deciding who would live there, who it would draw. I had never met Lou, but I knew the story that was told about those times. It was twelve years after he did this amazing thing that I came to be standing here. The county shut down Morningstar in 1971 after a controversial court battle and forced all the people living there to leave. Shortly after that, Lou's friend Bill Wheeler bought this place, eight miles or so from Morningstar. Many of the people who had to leave Morningstar ended up coming here, to Wheeler's. Bill didn't deed the land to God but declared it Open Land, which meant anyone could come and live here.

These really were acts of genius. Neither Bill nor Lou could have predicted or imagined what would follow.

I was one of those who heard the call. In 1967, when the court case was playing out in Sonoma County, California, debating the status of God's ownership of Morningstar, I was fourteen, a teenager in a small city in Oregon. I remember seeing on TV the nightly news reports by Walter Cronkite about the Vietnam War and the war protesters, about the civil rights marches, and about the hippies in Haight-Ashbury. They painted their faces with the words *love* and *peace*, and danced in the park, smiling at the TV cameras. They seemed to speak out about what was right and moral, unafraid to take on the world. I was intrigued by the free-spirited flower children, but I wasn't aware of the rampant drug use in the Haight and the toll it took on these young people. I wasn't mature enough to understand it all, but my world seemed tame and sheltered in comparison.

I had little to rebel against. I had a good family, great parents, a secure and stable home. But seeing the injustice in the world that I hadn't been aware of, I couldn't let go of that. I wanted to step out and see what the world was like — the world of the stories on the nightly news. I had a sense of social justice. I had a sense of curiosity and adventure. There was so much change going on in the world. I wanted to explore all that and understand more. Counterculture movements began to take hold that supported free speech, civil rights, women's rights, the environment, and the back-to-the-land movement. I watched and listened and absorbed all these things. I began to feel that my journey would not take the traditional path. These feelings laid the groundwork that would eventually lead me south to Wheeler's.

By 1978, I was at a point in my life when my too-young marriage had ended amicably and a business partnership had come to a natural close. I had spent the year before I left my hometown of Albany, Oregon, living in a tipi at my sister's rural home. That experience proved to be a primer for what lay ahead. But after a year of blissful tipi life, I took down the canvas and poles, sold them to a friend, and took to the road in my '66 Chevy Suburban. Betsy was a solid and reliable companion, originally a Forest Service vehicle. I learned how to do tune-ups on her, and how to change a tire, and I even once changed her fan belt with just the aid of a library book on car repair and some borrowed tools. I had a mattress and rugs in the back, and curtains on the windows. I just drove south and really had no idea where I was going.

Along my meandering journey, I stopped at hot springs, yoga retreats, and communes along the way. In those days, in the late 1970s, there were natural food stores and co-ops everywhere with notes on bulletin boards about places like that to go and stay. There grew to be a pattern when people I met at each stop told me that I should go to Wheeler's Ranch. I heard it over and over. "I can't just go there," I would answer. "No one has invited me. I don't know anyone there." Even when my reluctance was countered with, "Oh, it's Open Land, anyone is welcome," my response was still the same. "I can't just go there. Nobody has invited me." But something wanted me to go there. Something kept pulling me in that direction. The only way I would go, apparently, was if I had an invitation.

So fate created a path that would lead me to meet Bill Wheeler, the owner of the ranch. We met in a public hot tub at a place in Cotati called the Lotus Sutra. He invited me to the

ranch. Through that meeting with Bill, I now had directions and a personal invitation. After all the miles of my journey, and the mysterious suggestions by so many strangers whom I'd met on the road to go to Wheeler's Ranch, here it was, seemingly the obvious path to take. The destiny that had awaited me, had been calling me, now stood square in the middle of the road, luring me to it. Come to Wheeler's Ranch, it said.

But I didn't go. I rented a room in a house in Cotati about a twenty-minute drive from Wheeler's. Bill came by regularly, and we would go to the Lotus Sutra, or to the Mexican restaurant next to it, or he would take me to San Francisco in his old Cadillac. We would go out to some little Italian cafe, or play pool in a popular bar, or walk the city streets past San Francisco's legendary hippie landmarks, like the Haight-Ashbury district and the City Lights Bookstore. It was during this time that I started to discover, as Bill explained to me, what it was all about.

Bill was well known in the area. I had heard a little, but not much, about Wheeler's Ranch. I had a copy of Alicia Bay Laurel's book *Living on the Earth*, and it mentioned Wheeler's Ranch at the beginning. I had bought the book at Kiva, a bookstore in Eugene, Oregon, where I lived shortly after graduating from high school. I loved the book. But I didn't know anything about the history of Wheeler's Ranch or about all the amazing things that had happened there. I also didn't know why it kept coming up in my life, why I was being led there.

"Well," Bill said one day over pasta and a glass of Napa Valley cabernet, "most people around here know about the ranch." So he started to tell me the story from the beginning about how the ranch, and Morningstar before it, came to be.

"Lou Gottlieb," he said. "Amazing guy. Used to sing with the Limelighters. He bought a piece of land and deeded it to God. Called it Morningstar." He waited for that to sink in.

"Deeded it to God?" I said. "That's really interesting. I've never heard of anyone doing that."

I was intrigued, but Bill was at a loss. There was too much to tell. It was a bigger story than he could tell over a plate of pasta at an Italian restaurant. He looked off and took a deep breath, put his fork down, and took a sip of his wine. "Yeah," he said indignantly. "It was shut down!" he added, with some obvious raw emotion at the thought of it.

Both of us were silent for a minute. I couldn't react to a story I didn't know. He had lived through it and didn't know how to impress upon me all that had happened, and what it meant.

"You never heard of Wheeler's Ranch?" he asked again, still incredulous.

"Well, a little," I said. "I've heard the name. These last few months, wherever I've traveled, people kept telling me I should go to Wheeler's Ranch. And there was a book, I got it at a bookstore in Eugene, before I left Oregon. It's called *Living on the Earth* and it says at the beginning, 'Thanks to all the people at Wheeler's Ranch.' I love that book!"

"Yeah, that's Alicia's book," Bill said. "Alicia Bay Laurel. She lived at the ranch. She wrote it there. *Time* magazine even came out and interviewed her after the book was out. It was a big hit."

"Wow, Alicia Bay Laurel wrote that book at Wheeler's Ranch," I said, the wheels rotating in my brain. There was a reason things happened the way they did, I thought. I'd had that book, and little did I know that in the future, which was now, I'd be going there. I was getting more interested all the time.

Bill encouraged me again to come out to the ranch and see for myself. I decided I would go. So I followed the directions Bill had given me, and Betsy maneuvered her fat tires and rusty frame over the rutted dirt road, past Axle Creek and Oil Pan Rock (aptly named, for vehicles less durable than Betsy) and up to the front gate, where I parked her under the pine trees. I didn't know then that this was what had been drawing me. It would be eight years before I left.

2

> The world is but a canvas
> to our imagination.
> —Henry David Thoreau

It was a quiet and peaceful afternoon as I looked around at this new place I had come to. Betsy looked at home here. Even though she was in good shape, she was getting old and had a few dents and rusty spots, so she was in good company here, parked between a car that had no tires and a car that was covered with an inch of pine needles. We had been on the road for many miles, and I think we were both ready for a break. The sun shot rays of light through the tall pines, making a speckled pattern on the ground. I took my camera and a small backpack of clothes, and left Betsy to rest. Bill had told me to walk straight back on the main road until I saw his house on the right, next to a big garden and with a red roof.

This part of the road was wide enough for one car, barely, like the road heading in to where I had parked Betsy, and while bumpy and grooved it wasn't nearly as bad as the road coming down the hill. The only car that went down this part of the road most of the time was Bill's old Cadillac. Most people parked their car, if they had one, and walked in. There were flat grassy meadows on each side of the road, flanked by forests of big oaks and firs, and small brush. Then the road narrowed and the oaks on each side reached across and met in the middle, forming a shady canopy. I rounded a bend and a deer stood watching me, unafraid, and then two more came into view, grazing casually, unmoved by my presence there. Birds were calling from the trees and darting through the sky, and occasionally a hawk would come into view, soaring and gliding far above. It was so serene, not like a busy campground or public hiking trail, not like a farm or any of the rural roads like I'd grown up around, because it was so removed. The main road was a few miles back up the hill, and few people were likely to drive in unless they lived here, were invited, or just happened to hear about it, provided they had a vehicle that could make it or were willing to make the long trek on foot.

The first people I ran into on the road were a barefoot woman with long brown hair wearing a long tie-dyed skirt, a barefoot boy of about five with sweet brown eyes, and a man with Abe Lincoln legs in jeans and a denim jacket. They smiled when I asked, "Is this the road to Bill's house?" "Yep," the man said, "just keep going. You can't miss it." Soon, another young woman and a wild-haired man with a wheelbarrow full of freshly dug potatoes and carrots with the green tops still on, both bare chested and barefoot, walked by and smiled big at me. "I'm going to Bill's," I said, feeling like I had to explain why I was there. "Cool!" said the young woman, as they kept walking and talking over the banging and rattling of the wheelbarrow on the bumpy road. I looked at my feet. My boots weren't fancy, but they were fashionable and fairly new. They were good comfortable boots for walking in town. Here they suddenly seemed stiff and cumbersome. Everyone I passed was barefoot.

I saw a footpath going off into the trees and then another on the other side of the road, but I kept going straight on back where the road led and, as promised, came to Bill's house on the right. The large garden stretched out before the front porch. Chickens clucked and strutted and pecked the ground under a huge acacia tree, the neon yellow blossoms hanging like thick bunches of grapes. The tree was huge, the trunk massive and gnarled. The mass of yellow blossoms dominated a large part of the sky. Bill was standing at the front door of the wood-shingled two-story house with the red roof.

"Hey, you made it!" he said, welcoming me in. He put his arm around me. We had become good friends. I stepped in and looked around. The entire living space, which was most of the downstairs, was his studio. Two easels were set up, paintings stacked against the walls, brushes and tubes of paint on a table. I knew Bill was an artist. On one of our visits to San Francisco, he had taken me along to one of the life drawing classes at the Museum of Art. I knew that he hated for people to comment on his work, so I looked and admired the paintings but didn't say a word. I could see that much of his inspiration came from the land. The canvases featured the hills and trees, mountains and fields that I loved about the northern California landscape. There was a piano in the room, and a chessboard set up on the table as if someone had just been playing. There was an open bottle of wine on the kitchen counter. The small kitchen space looked out on the garden. Bill poured two glasses and we sat down to enjoy the day.

This first visit led to many more visits. I began coming out

every week, usually staying a few days at a time, and each time I would explore the paths and trails, and meet people who lived there. One path led to the back of the land, which was thick with pine trees that had been planted too close together, creating a stillness when standing in it, scented with pine. Another path led to the highest point on the land, which had been named Hoffy's Hill. I didn't know who Hoffy was, but I was sure he was one of the early hippie pioneers who had been here when Alicia wrote her book. It was a gently sloped and rounded hill that had a view of the surrounding ridges, and an opening between distant tall trees revealed the ocean just a few miles away. Other trails led to small cabins, each one tucked out of sight. I learned that at that time there were sixteen small cabins and three tents. These homes were all built by hand, mostly by the person living in them, and none of them had locked doors.

Bill had pretty much of an open-door policy at his house, and people felt welcome to drop by. Two visitors in particular were especially welcome—David and Mark. They both played the piano, which Bill encouraged. He didn't play himself but loved to hear David and Mark. David was from the East Coast and had grown up in a wealthy family, a musical prodigy who had played at Carnegie Hall as a child. Mark was from southern California, a born musician, a gift inherited from his father and grandfather in the family bloodline. He never took a lesson and could play just about anything. Mark and David were friends, and big fans of each other's music. David once told Mark, "I had to unlearn everything I'd been taught."

I liked them both, but Mark especially intrigued me. I had run into him a few times when I had come out to visit Bill. Not only was he talented, but he was also good looking and funny and brilliant. He didn't have a clue that I was interested in him. He thought I was off-limits, since I was sort of with Bill. But Bill and I were more like just friends.

I'll never forget the moment when I really connected with Mark for the first time. Bill was having a party, and the house was swirling with conversation, laughter, wine, food, and music, as parties do, and Mark was playing the piano in the midst of it. The melodies he was playing picked me up and carried me along, dimming everything else that was going on in the room. I was captivated, sitting behind Mark in a big easy chair, as he played. He didn't even realize I was there, and I just listened and was mesmerized by the music he was playing, and when the song came to a close and he lifted his fingers off the keys, it was as if I suddenly fell off a cloud and snapped back to the present moment. He turned around for a second and saw me, and I sighed and said, "Wow, that was really beautiful." He looked at me and realized I had been along for the ride. "Thank you," he smiled, and began playing again. Of all the people I had met at the ranch, maybe fifteen or so, he was the one I couldn't stop thinking about.

Valentine's Day rolled around, and Bill's ex-girlfriend showed up. Bill was hoping to get back with her, but there I was. Bill asked Mark to take me out to get me out of the way. I didn't mind. Before we left, another girl showed up to see Bill, a Canadian girl named Sheri. Bill asked Mark to take her too. So the three of us took Betsy, and I let Mark drive. We headed to a popular local club called the Inn of the Beginning, where Van Morrison was playing. Sheri was socializing on her own, and Mark and I were having fun dancing and talking. I was still very interested in him, and I could tell, especially when we were dancing, that he liked me. He loved Van Morrison and so did I. He told me he was thinking of buying a truck, and I was thinking of selling him Betsy. Our first "date," such as it was, was at the Inn of the *Beginning*. It seemed like an omen to me. I just had a feeling.

3

A garden to walk in and immensity to dream in—what more could he ask? A few flowers at his feet, and above him, the stars.
—Victor Hugo

There were three German visitors up by the front gate by the main road. I was heading into town, bringing back a bottle of Chardonnay from a local winery to share with Bill. He had invited me over for dinner. His ex-girlfriend had gone home. The Germans had seen a map on a bulletin board in a coffeehouse in Germany showing how to get to this place called Open Land. They didn't quite understand, and I wasn't much help, just starting to grasp it myself. But I knew how fortunate I was to have discovered it. I parked Betsy and got out for a minute to point the way.

From the high meadow where we stood, there was almost a bird's-eye view of the whole ridge, all a blue, green, and brown mosaic, with hazy purple patches of new redbud growth, and at the bottom of the canyons, the silver filigree of distant alders. Beyond it, the translucent coastal hills were layered like colored glass out to the horizon, where a deep blue streak of the Pacific Ocean melted into the robin's-egg blue of the sky. "It's just like the Ponderosa!" Anya sighed. They left their little foreign rental car at the edge of the field and set off down the hill on foot.

As I drove into town, I was aware of my conditioned desires to drive, to spend money, to go places, to buy things. I was a well-trained consumer. But the more often I visited here, and it was going on about six weeks now, I started to notice these things and how these desires had started to subside. That inner conflict was still in me, and it struggled with my desire to get back to the ranch. What a wonderland I had stumbled onto. I still marveled at the good fortune of being in this beautiful place. It was all I could think about while I was in town, and before long, Betsy and I were headed back up the winding narrow road. Since Betsy was one of the few vehicles that could easily make it down the rutted dirt road, it was as if she too belonged here. Finally, we were back, and it felt like being back home.

I started walking toward Bill's and decided to take a detour. Just before the path to Bill's there was a path through an old oak grove where Greg and Russ had built the "Cosmic Kitchen." They had used four small tree trunks as corner posts, to which was attached a canvas tarp, knotted at the top of the posts like a pirate's bandanna. There was a woodstove with a convoluted stovepipe strung from wires attached to overhanging branches. There were no walls, just a few shelves on three sides stacked with coffee cans and jars of rice, beans, grains, and popcorn. The stove was almost always going, except when everybody was asleep. People were always hanging out there, talking, eating, smoking, or just keeping warm by the stove.

As I approached, I heard voices. The German people had apparently stumbled upon it. Werner sat on a tree stump near where Mark was playing his guitar. He seemed mesmerized as Mark played lead riffs to something that was coming out of the little black radio by the woodstove. When the song was over, Werner smiled and shook his head. "I don't know how you do it, man," he said. "How can you just hear the notes and know where to play?" Mark smiled back at him. "It's hearing the notes that aren't there," Mark answered. "The invisible notes. Listen to the pauses." Werner shook his head. "I've been playing for years, and I can't do what you do. You're amazing! What are you doing out here? In the trees?" Mark tossed his head back, laughed, and continued playing.

Anya and Erhard were standing and talking with a few of the residents there, and the discussion was all about Open Land. The German visitors were confused, and everybody else was trying to explain it.

"Open Land means anyone can come and live here. No one really owns it," explained Ambriel. "Years ago, a guy named Lou Gottlieb deeded a place called Morningstar to God. But it was shut down when the courts decreed that God couldn't own land, because He couldn't walk into court and sign His name." She smiled, proud of the history that she had been through. "And so the people left Morningstar and came here. So even though it's Bill's land legally, he's actually sharing it. He declared it Open Land."

"It's tribal land," said Shahad solemnly. "In the sixties, some enlightened people got together and realized certain truths." He took a deep draw on the hash pipe and passed it to Anya.

"I think of it as an alternative community," Ambriel added, as the towheaded toddler she was watching hid his face in the folds of her gold print long skirt. "We live in separate houses, but we share roads, the water system, the garden, and we have a group sauna on Sundays. We celebrate holidays together like a family," she smiled.

"Nah," said Bob. "It's a human sanctuary. A retreat. It's a place for people who can't deal with the outside world."

I looked around at this assortment of people gathered together in this camp in the forest. Ambriel's red-haired son, Skye, sneaked up slowly on bent knees trying to catch one of Red's half-wild kittens. Red rubbed her scrawny yellow body against Erhard's leg and began purring. Greg, Russ, and Maggie were circled around the stove, pouring pancake batter onto the hot griddle. The three of them were naked except for their beaded bracelets and the three hawk feathers Maggie had braided into her hair. It was a hippie community and accustomed to casual nudity. Bob was the opposite in dress in his denim shirt and overalls, down jacket, and boots that looked capable of traversing glaciers. He opened his backpack and began taking out paperback books and stacking them on the wooden table. Mark sat at the edge of the group on a wooden bench, fine-tuning his guitar to the perfection of a discriminating ear.

Each of the Germans took a hit off the hash pipe that was passed around, and then Erhard said, "But what do you do here?"

"Anything you want!" laughed Maggie. "The only rule is . . . No Rules!"

"I don't know," said Russ, turning the pancakes on the griddle. "It's true, there's no rules here that everybody agrees on, but, well, there should be some kind of land trust. I mean, if that's really what it's about, then it should be legal. Otherwise, we're kind of at Bill's mercy. He could make us all leave if he wanted to."

"But there's been people living here almost ten years," countered Ambriel. "He's let people live here so long, there's a whole scene that's developed that has nothing to do with Bill. He has one vote at meetings, just like the rest of us. And there actually are a few rules that have evolved: watch your fires, bury your shit, and no dogs. There was a problem at one point with dogs because of all the wildlife and the neighboring sheep ranches," she grinned.

"No one could ever make me leave here," said Greg dreamily, pouring himself a cup of coffee. "I love this place like it's my own mother," he said to no one in particular, his eyes gazing upward in caffeinated rapture. "This place *is* my mother! I grow everything I need here, except coffee, olive oil, and Levis. I'm almost totally self-sufficient. I would never leave this place. I can't even imagine it!"

"This is a place to get in touch with nature," Mark said. "That's what it's all about."

4

He was a shooting star, brilliant in the vast sky full of bright lights in the darkness. His mission was clear and passionate and committed. It was a short flight, but amazing, magical, and unpredictable. I was a small flower in a field of flowers, opening slowly, changing from a bud full of potential into a fully bloomed creation, aware of my shyness in the crowded grassy field, aware of my smallness, and my sacred place in the world. I knew that after I bloomed, I would slowly shrivel, send out seeds of what I had been, and then silently merge back into the ground that had born all of us flowers. But that one night, I looked up and saw my shooting star, and I was enchanted. I knew I had seen my true love.

From the first time I heard Mark playing piano at Bill's, I was intrigued. The blind date Bill had set us up on had cemented my feelings even more. There was something about him. He had a flirtatious charm, a genuine smile, and a great laugh—hearty, spontaneous, and real. Certainly his musical talent impressed me. Sometimes when I'd see him walking on the road, he would be singing, or he'd pull out a pen and start writing notes on his arm, if he was without paper, to remind himself of key lyrics or chords until he got to a guitar or piano to play a new song that had come to him. He was pretty humble about his talent. Once Bill had said to me, after Mark had been playing piano at his house, that Mark had more talent in his little finger than anyone, and that even though others had access to the best schools in the world, you couldn't buy what Mark was born with. He didn't let Mark hear it, but later I told Mark what Bill had said. Mark felt very moved by that.

I had a flash once, after he had passed me on the road, that he reminded me of a movie character I'd had a crush on in my adolescent years, Billy Bigelow in the movie *Carousel*. Billy Bigelow was the charming bad boy that the good girl, played by Shirley Jones, fell in love with. Mark had a bit of that bad boy charm. He even looked a little like Billy Bigelow, with his dark wavy hair and his solid but graceful build. They even wore the same style of Greek fisherman's cap. Mark told me he had found the hat on the main road after a sports car convertible rushed by and the guy's hat flew off. He didn't come back for it, so Mark picked it up. It looked good on him.

I kept coming out to visit the ranch more and more, and really feeling like I didn't want to leave. I started getting to know some of the other people who lived there. I would see Molly walking along with her five-year-old son, Victor, and Del, always in denim, who I came to find out was an artist and a poet. These three were the ones I had first encountered on my initial visit. I'd talk to Bob walking in from town with his backpack filled with books, or I'd sit with David in the garden or up on Hoffy's Hill. David always wore a clean white shirt, clean white pants, and clean white tennis shoes even though the only laundry facilities were a bucket, an outdoor faucet, and a little soap. I'd hear stories about people who used to live there and about the early Morningstar settlers who had moved there after Morningstar was shut down. They were like legends now to those of us who followed.

I heard stories from Bill and Mark and David about how this community at Wheeler's itself had been shut down and everyone forced to leave. That story held a lot of emotion, for Bill especially. It's the history to my story, but one I can't tell firsthand. My arrival at Wheeler's was like the third wave. From what I heard, it seemed that after Morningstar, there was a momentum created that could not be stopped. Everyone who had been there had tasted a new kind of freedom, a new way of living close to the earth, in "voluntary simplicity." A movement had been born and the people were like seeds cast out to take root in new soil. It was a hard thing to suppress, as if it was responding to a higher law. Both Morningstar and Wheeler's were wild, uncharted territory where people were learning how to live on the land and how to live with each other. The only rules that evolved were: bury your shit, watch your fires, and no violence. Similar communities began to spring up across the country.

The more visits I made, the more I wanted to stay. It wasn't long before I wished I had my own place there, and when I mentioned it to Mark, he said there might be something available coming up. We were both leaving Bill's after Mark and David had provided us with an impromptu piano concert.

"So, how do I go about it?" I asked Mark as we walked along. "If I wanted to stay here and live, could I do that? Do I ask Bill?"

"It's kind of unwritten, since the community's been shut down before, and at times, there's just been way too many people. But now, well, you just need to wait until a house site comes available, and ask around," Mark answered. "It's not really up to Bill. He declared it Open Land, so just see if anybody objects, and figure out a way to get by. It's almost like a rite of passage, to make your own shelter and learn to rely on yourself if you're going to live here. Hoti just left, and he had a tent on a platform right up this way. I'll show it to you. He said he was giving it to me, but that's not exactly how it works, and I already have a place. His place is right up here on the left."

We walked a little farther under the ceanothus trees, the wild California lilac, that flanked the dirt road on both sides. The lavender blossoms smelled like honey. We got to a small open meadow and the hill gradually sloped down from there to the west. Mark turned off onto a well-traveled path. I followed, excited at what I might find. The path made a gradual, gentle descent as it wove through a sparse forest of small shrubs, a few small ceanothus, and a few firs. Before long, we came to a little clearing in the forest and I saw the wooden platform and the tent under a huge, beautiful bay tree. I noticed a faucet about 10 feet from the tent.

"So I could move in here then?" I asked, in awe. "And actually live here?"

"Well, probably, yeah," Mark said, "if nobody objects. You should ask Larry and Byron, they're the closest neighbors—they've got a cabin right over there," and he motioned toward the direction we had come from. I hadn't seen anything, but apparently there were neighbors. "And check with the knoll, that's the ridge across the canyon. There's three ladies living

just across the canyon, over that way," and he motioned to it, and again, I didn't see anything but the forest. "So just ask around, and if you can make it happen, it's yours. I'm sure Bill won't mind."

From one direction, I heard the sound of a metal pan and water from a faucet hitting it, and then footsteps on wood. I heard distant voices from across the canyon. There were neighbors out there, hidden in the forest, even though I couldn't see them.

Wow, no down payment or deposit. No rent. No papers to fill out and sign. No application. No landlord. Just ask around and see if anybody minds if you move in. I knew from that moment that a new era in my life was about to begin. I had never run into a situation like that. I hadn't even known it existed. It was almost unthinkable. But there it was. A free place to live in the woods. Just ask if anybody objects.

When I talked to Bill, he seemed pleased, but he told me I should check with the community, and especially those who would be the nearest neighbors. So I talked to Larry and Byron, David, and Ambriel. They all said it would be fine. It's Open Land, I would hear. Anyone is welcome, unless it gets to the point where there's too many. But even then, there weren't any rules to address that, and since I was taking a spot that someone else had moved out of, it wasn't an issue. I asked everyone I saw, and no one had any objections. No one even seemed to feel that I needed to ask.

When I saw Mark and told him everyone seemed to approve of my moving into Hoti's abandoned tent, he seemed as pleased as Bill had. He had lived at Wheeler's for two years, and he told me how grateful he was every day to be living there.

"I've been writing so much since I moved here," he told me. "Hundreds of songs. It's like a muse. Sometimes it's like there's a radio playing in my head. I just hear these songs, and I never take it for granted."

"Is that why you moved here?" I asked. "To write?"

"Well, initially I moved here to get a break from the L.A. music scene. I got tired of playing in bands that hired girls in black lipstick to scream for us. I just needed a change. So my brother Greg told me about this place, and I came to visit him, just because it was a place to go, and I just never left. It's a pretty incredible place."

"Greg's your brother?" I said. They were nothing alike, more like exact opposites.

"Yeah, well, I don't advertise it. We don't get along. The only decent thing he's ever done for me is tell me about this place," Mark said.

Greg was a little strange, even in this group. He rarely left the land for months at a time. His hair always looked wild, and he rarely combed it. He rarely wore anything except a pair of old cut-off jeans. He worked like a maniac in the garden and bragged about how much he had done, sometimes posting long itemized lists of his efforts and accomplishments on the bulletin board. He could be kind and generous one minute, and volatile or vengeful the next. I had heard stories about him, too, and I wasn't surprised by what Mark said about his brother. But he was one of the first to move here after the previous shutdown, and he was totally committed to living off the land. People respected him for that, even though he alienated others socially. Greg didn't mind if I moved in and asserted that it was Open Land and anyone could live there. Neither did anyone else I asked have any objections. So I moved in.

5

Great Solitude—hath one thousand voices and a flood of light. Be not afraid. Enter the Sanctuary. Thou will be taken by the hand and led to Life's own fountain!
—Queen Elizabeth of Romania,
from a Celestial Seasonings tea box

When I was in the tent I had inherited, I felt totally safe. There was such a sense of peacefulness here. There were no bears or cougars or wolves, or poisonous snakes, or any animal I would need to be afraid of. The bigger animals, the raccoons, bobcats, deer, kept to themselves, and except for the deer, were heard but rarely seen.

There were no people I needed to worry about breaking in. Rarely did anyone come who wasn't a guest of someone's or a previous resident who knew the scene, and no car could easily drive in. Even if some random person walked in, they wouldn't really notice or follow the little hidden footpaths that led to homes. The place felt protected by both its natural barriers and the peaceful presence that permeated the atmosphere. It just felt good being there.

The tent was used but clean, and the wooden platform it was on was solid and kept the tent floor off the ground. It was tall enough to stand up in and had room for a bed and a chair and some storage, maybe even a little camp stove. There was a little garden that Hoti had fenced with some dilapidated old chicken wire. It wasn't real sturdy. Mark told me that Clarabelle, the old cow that roamed the land, had already pushed the fence down once since I'd been there, and he had propped it back up. The garden had a fragrant jasmine vine with whitish-pink flowers that climbed all across the top of the fence and was thickest by the gate, so you were enveloped in its wonderful aroma as you squeezed past it to go in. There were three small raised beds around the edges, and a wooden platform in one corner, big enough to sleep on.

I liked the thought of sleeping in a garden under a blooming jasmine and tall fir trees. Small leaves of spinach, scraggly and dry from neglect, struggled to stand up in the sandy soil, but the rosemary, sage, and oregano were still full and thriving. I loved sitting on the platform in this little garden, smelling the jasmine and dreaming of what I could plant there right outside my door. The water faucet was close enough that the piece of old garden hose that Hoti had left was sufficient to spray the thirsty plants.

Once I got the approval of the community, the approval that everyone told me I didn't really need, I settled in. I made up my bed in the tent, and another one in the garden. I brought my cooking supplies and dishes and utensils, my battery-operated lantern and candles and matches, my sleeping bag, a couple of sheets and blankets, a few washcloths and towels, and some wooden boxes to make into shelves. I wasn't yet set up to do much cooking, but I was invited to join others for meals, and it was a good way to get to know people.

It felt so right. This place had been waiting for me, and I thought about all the things that had led me here, and I knew this was where I wanted to be. That first evening, before I went to bed, I sat outside for a while, just thinking. It was still and very quiet. I didn't even hear any neighbors. My mind was racing around like a wild stallion with too much room to run. There was a sense of both physical and mental freedom here. I noticed how my mind jumped around trying to fill space. I wasn't used to having that much space and solitude. I was used to the sounds of clocks, and people, and traffic, and activity. Now there were no TV shows marking increments of thirty minutes, and no blaring commercials.

My mind was in a big vacuum with more freedom and space than it was used to. I sat quietly and let my mind wander as far as it wanted to go. When the stars came out, I looked up and marveled at my good fortune. The bright stars were so thick in the black sky, and so magical. My thoughts dissipated into a vast stillness. I was more than ready, and willing, to lie down in my new home and dream. I climbed into the comfy bed I had made out of blankets and a sleeping bag, and closed my eyes.

That very first morning when I woke up after having officially moved in, with no plans to hit the road again, the magic was still there. The spell had not worn off. I lay there and savored that first daybreak, with the stillness of the woods outside and the birds chirping into the new day. The rising morning sun made the canvas tent glow. I stretched and breathed deep and looked around. I had slept so well. I could see the trees outside through the door flap that hung open. I can live here, I thought. I can *live* here. I can live *here*. When had I ever awakened and found myself with a whole free day and a space to be in without owing anybody anything for being there? I actually lived here now.

I pulled out my journal and wrote these words. Then I walked out to the faucet and splashed water on my face and ran my fingers through my hair. I pulled on my jeans and the same cotton shirt I'd worn the day before, and barefoot, headed up the path. I knew I was at the beginning of a very special journey. As I walked up the trail from my tent, the sun was just coming up over Joy Ridge. I stood there and took it in. I kept reminding myself I could live here as long as I wanted. It was quiet. No one nearby seemed to be up.

I went back to my tent and got a blanket and came back and spread it out in a clearing where there was a flat space. It was totally private, a round grassy space surrounded by coyote bushes and small ceanothus trees. I sat down, cross-legged, facing the sun. Breathing deeply, I meditated and flowed through a series of yoga poses. My mind felt so clear. This was indeed a special place, and I couldn't stop marveling at my being there. Not just being there, but living there, and with no obligation.

After a while I got up, raised my hands and bowed my head to the sun one more time, and took a deep breath. It was time to explore. I headed off up the road, toward Tiara's Hill. It couldn't have been a more beautiful day. The hill was a blanket of tall waving grasses. I started to walk up the small hill toward a point where I could look back and see the entire ridge that composed Wheeler's Ranch. We often saw deer up here grazing, especially in the morning.

I never knew until I lived here what a deer sounds like. They have a voice unlike any other animal I've ever heard. They talk in varying tones of whistles and whooshing sounds, like heavy breathing.

I was looking down at my steps when I heard it. A giant

exhale. Whoosh. I looked up. There were three male deer with antlers standing across the crest of the hill just in front of me. I was stunned. We had seen only females and babies, or one male with a few females, but this was three males with antlers. I could tell by the size of their antlers and their bodies that this was three distinct generations.

The grandfather deer had bulky, leathery folds around his neck. He was the biggest of the three and had a dark, thick coat and well-established muscles. His antlers were huge and majestic, and he carried them on his head like a royal crown. The middle-sized deer, possibly the grandfather deer's son, was a perfectly formed and beautiful animal in his own right, but neither he nor the smaller deer could match the powerful confidence of the grandfather deer.

We had startled each other. I wasn't watching where I was going, and suddenly there they were. The smallest deer, his antlers not yet fully formed, turned immediately when he saw me, pranced two or three steps away, and then looked back at the other two. He was ready to run if given the signal.

The middle-sized deer jerked his head, pranced a little without retreating, and twitched his tail. He looked at me, then looked quickly away.

The grandfather deer stood there posed like a lord in his kingdom. He faced me straight on, right where he was standing. He held his head high and kept unwavering eye contact with me. He was neither frightened nor aggressive. All I could do was stare. I had never seen anything like him. Then, when he was ready, he flew by me into the nearby trees and vanished. The other two, already waiting close to the trees, followed him and left me standing there, still in awe.

6

> The Cosmos is in us. We are made of star stuff. We are a way for the Universe to know itself.
> —Carl Sagan

Even though I'd been visiting the ranch for a couple months, on my first official day of actually living there I almost didn't know what to do with myself. It was amazing to have that kind of opportunity, when my options were so open I didn't even know where to start. Seeing the three deer on the hill had been an amazing start to my morning. I had stood there for a while after the deer ran off, just looking over the ridge, and then when I walked back down the hill, I ran into David and breathlessly told him what I had seen. He was surprised, and delighted with my story. He had been there almost longer than anybody else and hadn't seen that.

I loved hearing about all the people who

lived there now or had lived there before. Every day now I had the freedom to just walk along the road and be. So I walked, and sat and talked to people I ran into.

I was intrigued by O.B. Ray. He was one of the ones who had lived at Morningstar. Everybody knew who he was. He rose early every morning to hike to the bottom of the East Canyon or to the top of Tiara's Hill, or around Sugarloaf Mountain to the main road. His long fuzzy gray hair merged with the well-kept long gray beard under his chin. He was distinguished by his Irish nose and apple cheeks, his dark eyes set in continuous lines of laughter, and his ever-present pipe. I had seen him often in brown overalls, a turtleneck shirt, and a small backpack. Every day he hiked to the top of the hill or the bottom of the canyon, where he filled his pipe and sat in silence, a Zen master contemplating whatever it was he was contemplating, or thinking nothing at all. He had been many things in his life, a cabdriver, a father of five, and had spent years in a monastery studying and translating ancient Sanskrit texts. He had given one of these books to Mark, and Mark told me about him. It was not O.B.'s policy to get involved in anyone's arguments, and he didn't go to any meetings or vote on any decisions that were put to a vote. Meetings and voting were pretty infrequent there anyway, but it wasn't his way. He had his pipe to share, and his laughter, which rang out over the hills wherever he was, so you always knew when he was around and who he was visiting. His deep and hearty laugh was easily recognized and was often followed by the sound of coughing, which indicated that he was passing the pipe.

David was another favorite of mine. He was a good friend of Mark's and of Bill's, and was welcome at everyone's house. He usually had a big fat joint, a warm smile, and a twinkle in his eye. He visited everyone and became somewhat of a news carrier. If you wanted to find out something, David would probably know, and he might tell you. If you wanted to spread the word about a party, David would do it.

I loved the completeness of this community in the hills. We had not only our own water supply and a full garden but also entertainment, musicians and story tellers, and neighbors to visit with, and cooks and craftsmen and painters and poets.

Russ had arrived not long before me. He had long red hair, and an athletic build, fair skin, and lots of freckles. In another time, he could have been a Viking. He had that look. He was trying to live off the land completely and at one point wore just a knitted skirt and a poncho that he made himself, and he bought two donkeys to carry stuff. He didn't ride in a car and he said that sometimes when he was in town, tourists would want to take his picture. He stopped brushing his long hair until it got matted like felt. Then he had Maggie embroider on it and planned to cut it off and make a hat from his own hair.

Two guys from San Francisco lived next door to me, Larry and Byron, and they were really nice and pleasant to visit. There was only one family there at the time, and that was Molly and Del and Victor. There were a few other guys from San Francisco, Dean, who often dressed in a loincloth, moccasins, braids, and beaded headbands, and Tommy, who was a master carpenter and dressed in a cowboy hat and boots. They were close friends.

Jeannie and Charles were two others who had been at Morningstar whom I was just getting to know. Mark knew them well, and they both welcomed me at their homes. Bob lived in a tent in the pine forest at the back of the land and started a library back there. He hitchhiked into the city and bought used books, mostly paperback, until he had acquired about two hundred books on various subjects—classics, fiction, nonfiction, kids' books, mysteries, religious studies. He made long bookcases three shelves high that encircled his own overstuffed and worn living room chair, and he had several folding chairs, and stools, and a couple of wooden boxes to sit on. A tarp was strung up over it because the library was always open, even in the rain, and had become a social gathering place. The only walls were the walls of books, and all around, just pine trees.

Clarabelle and Sweetheart, two cows that had been cast off from local farms, wandered freely. Clarabelle was said to be too short to be bred, and Sweetheart, too tall. So they lived there, and Greg would go look for them with his milk pail once a day. He and Maggie drank the milk and made butter and shared it with others. Bill's sheep, Lammy Bammy, followed Clarabelle because she had been raised on Clarabelle's milk. Clarabelle was pretty docile, but Sweetheart had horns and a bad habit of pushing down garden fences. Eventually she got sent back to the farm she had come from, but not before she taught Clarabelle her bad behavior of breaking into poorly fenced gardens.

Another sheep, named Clyde, also joined the family. He impressed me because he had come across the canyon from Star Mountain of his own free will. Star Mountain, a community similar to Wheeler's, raised sheep and sheared them for their wool, which Jade and Delia and Phyllis made into hats and scarves and sold in local shops. But Star Mountain also had a large freezer at the main house that was filled with lamb chops and mutton steaks. That's why I was impressed by Clyde's escape across the canyon. Wheeler's Ranch was mostly vegetarian. There were no freezers full of lamb chops at Wheeler's. I think somehow Clyde knew that. Even a sheep knew that this was a special place.

I was beginning to walk barefoot most of the time now. The paths were soft and dusty in the summer and gooshy after a light rain. The earth was kind even to vulnerable feet, with cool grass in patches here and there, and very few rocks or thistles where we walked. Each time I headed down the road on foot, when I got near the Cosmic Kitchen, the smell of wood smoke and buckwheat pancakes would inevitably tempt me, especially knowing that there would be homemade butter and pure maple syrup to go with it. As I approached, I could hear Greg, Maggie, and Russ talking. Maggie had a paperback book on her lap and a joint in her hand. "Check it out, Joy," she said, smiling. "It's a copy of *The Morningstar Scrapbook*. There aren't too many of these around!"

"What is it?" I asked, looking over her shoulder.

"Ramon and Coyote and a bunch of those guys, they put this together and printed up some copies with photos of when Morningstar got started. It tells the whole story of all these people coming there, and how they started building little shacks and lean-tos. The court case, and everything. Oh, look!" She pointed at one of the pictures. "It's Rena! She was with Lou."

"Wow, what a cool book," I said. "It's got news clippings too. Can I borrow it?"

"Sure," Maggie said, handing me the worn and tattered book. "You know, these guys were the trailblazers. This is what led us to where we are now!"

"And here we are," said Russ, turning pancakes on the griddle. "It's pretty amazing. Here, Joy, you can have these," he said, handing me a plate of pancakes.

"I just made that butter this morning," said Greg, emptying the last of the coffee into his cup.

I spread the butter on the warm pancakes, poured on the maple syrup, sat down on a log stump, and took a bite. "Mmmm," I said. "These are so good. Every time I smell them I can't resist stopping by."

"Don't resist!" Maggie said. "We've been making them every day!"

7

> Do you want to love somebody?
> Let it be me.
> —Mark

Ours was not an instant, linear track of falling in love. The path Mark and I were led down was a wandering, zigzagging path, maybe even with both of us dragging our feet. We had each been through a breakup much too recently to be looking for love again. He had left southern California after breaking up with his high school sweetheart. My early and young marriage had ended in an inevitable and amicable divorce a little more than a year before I came to the ranch. But there was a spark between us that was undeniable.

I was much more interested in him than he was in me. That's why it surprised me when he invited me to his cabin.

He had built his place farther down the side

of the ridge than anyone else except Jeannie, who lived in a previously established house site almost all the way to the bottom of the canyon. Her place had a wide, well-traveled path that led there and then went on to the creek at the bottom of the East Canyon. Mark's trail was barely visible. He left it obscure because he wanted the privacy, regularly pushing piles of leaves across it to cover the visible marks made by his footsteps. He had shown me the beginning of the trail, and from there it was less a trail than a path of least resistance. I went cautiously, step by step, wherever a branch didn't poke me in the eye. I wasn't even sure I was on the trail. Of the twenty-five people living there at the time, only a handful had found his place.

But I kept going, and after a slow downward hike of about ten minutes, I saw the corner of his roof revealed between the trees. I had found it. I called out to him. No answer. A little way farther and I stepped closer to the porch. I called again. No answer.

I was not surprised to see that his house was as unique as he was. The porch and one side of the house was about seven feet above the ground, the other sides of the house having been built right into the side of the hill. The windows danced around the sides and were not even—some were not even straight and looked like musical notes playing across sheet music. The house faced a small grove of tall redwoods at about the middle of the trees' height. I loved it.

I knocked and called again. Maybe he was outside nearby. Still no answer. I don't know what possessed me, but I went in. Maybe it was because it took so much to get there. And he had invited me. To this day, I don't remember ever having gone into someone's house when they weren't home, especially someone I had just met. But here, no one had locks on their doors. I felt invited. So I went in to wait.

There was a woodstove, a small table with two chairs,

candles, and some shelves with kitchen utensils. There was a little bronze Buddha that held a stick of incense, and a teardrop-shaped crystal hanging in the window that shot rainbows around the room. The bed was built up on tall posts, tall enough to store his guitar and personal things underneath in baskets and boxes, but not too tall to climb onto. Like all the other places on the ranch, the walls had wood siding that didn't match.

Even as high up as it was, with the seven-foot drop below the porch, the house felt rock solid. The view across the East Canyon revealed the neighboring ridge, coincidentally named Joy Ridge. The open area outside the front door and the steep slope of the hill above the house formed a circular space much like an open amphitheater that even a non-musician like me could see was perfect for acoustics. The house was clean, swept, and uncluttered. It felt good being there.

I waited about twenty-five minutes, and it was starting to get dusky. I hoped he would get back soon, since I was pretty sure I wouldn't be able to find my way back up the hill if it started to get dark. I hopped up on the bed and waited. I'd give it a few more minutes. He had invited me, and I really wanted to see him.

Then I heard him coming down the hill. He was singing. As he opened the front door, I hopped off the bed and stood there. He saw me in the shadows of the darkened room and hit the roof.

"What are you doing here? What do you . . . you just come in my house? Whaddya think you're doing?!!" He was irate.

Guilt crept over me. What was I doing? "I'm sorry!" I said, walking toward the door, "I'm sorry! I shouldn't have, I know, but it took a long time to get here, and . . . and . . . I'm sorry, I'll leave."

We were both standing near the door now, and I was out of the shadows and into the window light. Now he could see me. He recognized my voice when I spoke. He breathed a sigh of relief and put his hand up to stop me from going out the door. "Joy, it's you, stay. Please. I didn't know it was you. I thought you were that other girl, what's her name." He looked noticeably pleased now.

"You mean Erica?" I said.

"Yeah," he said shaking his head. "She's been hounding me all day. I finally lost her, and no, really, I'm glad it's you. Sit down."

He smiled finally, and we both laughed. I had no explanation for walking into his house when he wasn't home, but it didn't matter now. Mark lit some candles and pulled back the curtains. The dark redwoods stood in shadow against the distant hills. "Did you check out the view?" he said.

"Yeah, it's amazing."

"Those three redwoods out there are the only three redwoods on the ranch. There must have been a lot of them hundreds of years ago, but they were probably all logged, and those three are the only ones left. That's one of the reasons I chose this spot."

"I love your place," I said. "It's got five sides, and none of them are the same length! I think I remember from grade school, isn't that a trapezoid?" I smiled, looking around.

"Probably!" He laughed. "I had a great time building it. I just made it work. And you know, even though it's not a typical square house, the roof has never leaked. Not a drop! Some of the other houses here have had leaky roofs, but it's never leaked. I love it here."

He pulled his guitar out from under the bed, opened the case, and sat on the bed with the guitar across his lap. All of the windows were open, swung out on hinges, and the outlines of the trees were silhouettes now against the dim glow of the evening sky. The last rays of sun reached across the front porch, and Joy Ridge lit up in green and gold patches across the canyon.

"I've been working on a new song," Mark said, tuning up the strings. "That's another reason I chose this spot. The acoustics are great down here, and no one else is within hearing range, so I can sing and play all night if I want to. Except Jeannie. Once in a while she yells across at me, if it's late, but I don't really care!"

"There's worse things than hearing music through the trees," I agreed.

So he played the new song, and another, and another. It was heaven. I loved everything he played.

Eventually we made a small fire in the woodstove, just enough to take the chill off and melt some cheese onto the tortillas he had brought back from town. We laughed again about me walking into his house when he wasn't home, and him thinking at first that I was Erica.

After that night, I knew that even though Bill had brought me to the land, Mark was the one I was destined to meet. We started spending more and more time together. Bill wasn't crushed—he had plenty of women in his life. There were other women interested in Mark, too, but even though I had some competition, Mark kept looking me up. We could talk about anything. He always had something interesting to say. He was brilliant, and well-informed about the world, usually having a different perspective no one else had thought of. He also kept me laughing. He loved puns, and he loved satire. He had a great sense of humor, and I got it. We were somehow in tune with each other's thoughts.

I didn't want to be tied down, but Mark didn't seem to be the settling-down type. I couldn't imagine him ever being predictable or ordinary.

Coming from Oregon, I was different from the girls Mark had known in L.A. It took me a while to realize that he liked that about me. Even in a counterculture environment, I felt embarrassingly wholesome in the hip world of California. In Oregon, I was seen as a free spirit. I had lived in a tipi, which many of my family members found strange but intriguing. I had opened the first natural food store in my hometown and taught a yoga class. And I looked like a hippie with my long hair, beads, patched jeans, embroidered peasant blouse, and little or no makeup. In Oregon, hippies weren't all that common in the early seventies outside of Eugene. But here in California, I felt naive, unworldly, and sheltered in comparison to others I met. I didn't realize until I traveled far from home that having a stable and loving family as a foundation wasn't the norm everywhere. Mark liked hearing about my family and seeing my excitement when I got letters from home. I talked more openly about myself when I was alone with him than when I was feeling shy in a crowd. He didn't mind my shyness, either. He was outgoing enough for both of us. "You're different from other girls, Joy," he said. "You should embrace that."

He was different from other guys, too. He had an intense commitment to personal freedom, a trait I wished more people had. He wrote an anthem about freedom that I loved to hear him sing.

Gonna do what I want,
gonna say what I feel,
oh yeah,
takin' my time.

Gonna live how I want,
how I see as real,
made up my mind,
no big deal.

Don't try to tell me I'm wrong,
try to say what's fair for me.

Someday I'll die, who knows
what tomorrow will be,
let me live my life in peace,
give it all a chance.

Don't give a damn
what the papers are saying,
all the trash that they're always displayin'.
Don't give a damn about no politician
trying to sell me the official position.

(guitar lead)
Say what I feel
(guitar lead)
Gonna do what I want

I had heard him play both piano and guitar. He was amazing. He wrote beautiful heartfelt ballads and love songs, wild hard rock, magical classical instrumentals, and hilarious songs that were funnier because of the comical voice he sang them in.

I knew a hooligan, Floogle McDougal.
McDougal McDuff said he'd poop on my poodle.

And he wrote instrumentals inspired by deep thoughts, and by people and places he had lived—"La Mirada," "Joy," "Springtime Sheep Ridge," "Blue Flower Spring," and "Speculation on Times Yet to Come," which has a melody every bit as mystical and evocative as the title suggests.

8

Water is the gold of the future.
—Vernon Pinard (Mark's dad)

The winter rains had swelled the stream that washed down the hill, carrying silt and fine mud along with it. The pond was so heavily filled in with silt, it was half its former size. It was to be expected. It happened every year, naturally, and once the rains seemed to be pretty much over, the silt needed to be scooped out of the pond so it had its usual holding capacity. Cleaning out the pond was one of the fun jobs. It wasn't uncommon to have too much help.

It had to be a warm, sunny day because you had to strip down and stand in the pond naked. That's the way it was done. Some people just wore cut-offs, but you were going to get covered with mud anyway. When Mark and I arrived, Larry, Byron, Jeannie, David, and Ambriel were all standing in the pond, naked and streaked with mud from the neck down. They all had five-gallon plastic buckets and were scooping the water out, handing the full buckets along in a bucket brigade to Greg and Dean and Nathan standing on the banks. Mark and I took off our clothes and climbed in. They had already made progress. The water was at about thigh level. Once it was empty, we could start digging out the silt.

"Hey, you guys are too clean!" Byron said, smiling, as he dumped a bucket of muddy water on me.

"Aaah!" I screamed, even though it felt refreshing.

"You too, Mark," laughed Ambriel as she scooped a handful of mud and streaked it across his chest. At the same time, Nathan tossed muddy water on his back. "Woah! Enough!" Mark said in defense.

We joined the line, and Mark scooped the bucket full of water and passed it to me. I grabbed it with both hands from underneath as he swung it up and it passed then to Ambriel, and we both helped to lift it up to Greg, who poured it off into the bushes a few feet away. He tossed the empty bucket back to Mark and we started again. We formed three bucket brigade lines and the water went down rapidly. We were in a relaxed and easy synchronization that made the work go smoothly.

The scooping action of the buckets created waves. The water splashed brown muddy splotches onto our arms, our bodies, our faces. The mud we were standing in was soft and slick, and we were up to our ankles. Now and then we ducked into the cool water before it got too shallow, and then another splash of mud tattooed its muddy designs on us, and the mud-caked buckets smudged mud on whatever part of us they touched. We looked like a Stone Age tribe in some kind of mud bath ceremony. It felt good. We were having a good time, working together, and resting when we needed to.

Finally the water was all bailed out. Now we had to dig out

the silt. It was heavy and we could fill the buckets only part way. Larry and Mark brought shovels and took one side, while our bucket brigade was on the other. The ground around the pond looked ugly with the silt piled on top of plants, but we knew it wouldn't take long before they grew back through it. We had been at it for about forty minutes, and the sun was getting higher and warmer. The sparse leaves of the wild lilac leaned over the pond, sheltering us from direct sun. How nice the cool water would feel now, I thought, standing in the drained pond.

Finally the silt was dug out to where the natural perimeters of the pond started, the harder ground indicating the pond was back to its original size. The water was already starting to trickle in. "That seems about right," Larry said, surveying the project. We all agreed. It was a job well done. Now we just had to wait about twenty-four hours for it to fill in again with water from the uphill stream, and then a little bit longer for the silt to settle and the water to clear in the pipes. We had all saved buckets of water to use during this time.

We climbed out of the muddy pond and walked up the trail to the road. One by one we emerged, single file, from below the wooded hill, all of us naked and covered with mud. As we reached the dirt road, a brand new Volvo, unfamiliar to us, drove up. I was wondering how he got it down the road, since we never saw cars down there except for the few trucks that a few people had. This guy must not have known what the road was like and then couldn't turn back. We were all talking among ourselves, wondering who he was and why he was here. The Volvo slowed down and then stopped. The driver looked at us as we walked up casually, pleasantly exhausted and covered with mud. He turned off his car and got out. He was wearing a suit and tie and dressy black shoes.

"Is this the road to Bill's?" he said, not acknowledging the fact that we are all naked and muddy.

"Yeah, right down this road, and when the road forks, go to the right. It's the first house you'll see," Mark directed him. The man looked down the road the direction Mark had pointed, and when he looked back, three more naked muddy people had walked out of the trees.

"Thanks," he said. "Just right down this road and then take the right fork?"

"You can't miss it!" Larry assured him.

The guy got back into his car and started off down the road, slowly steering into the ruts instead of over them. The Volvo groaned as it dipped and climbed and rocked its way along. We were well aware of how odd we must have seemed to him, but we hadn't said anything to explain our appearance. Watching him drive off, suddenly we all laughed.

"I guess we surprised him!" Jeannie said. "What were the chances that he drove by at that moment? He had obviously never been down this road before."

All of us headed to our own space to wash up. We had buckets of water set aside to use. By the next morning the pond would be settled and refilled. Cal would get the pump running so that the water was pumped up to a holding tank that was higher than all of our houses. That way we used only gravity to send it down to each of our homes. The pond just happened to be lower than most of our building sites, thus the need for the pump. This was our water system, built before I moved there but maintained even now by those of us who wanted to maintain it.

A water marshall was chosen, currently Larry. I was thrilled that I got to be part of the water crew, and that I was shown what to do and how to fix breaks in the line. It was a good system and provided us with all the water we needed. If the

water got low in summer, we'd put out the word that the pond was low, and we'd all voluntarily limit our use until it filled up again. Simple and sustainable. And we didn't have to pay anybody for the water.

Mark was the only person on the ranch who had his very own water system. He had found a spring and purposely built his house below it so he could have gravity flow water. He carefully dug a beautiful little pond about a foot and a half deep and four feet across. The water came right up out of some rocks and flowed gently into the pond just below. From there he ran a pipe down the hill about twelve feet, where he put a faucet adjacent to his front porch. The water was so clear and tasted so pure. Mark loved the notion that it was likely no one had drunk from it for probably a hundred years or so. The land had previously been used for sheep ranching before the communal scene came along, and the spring was too far down the hill and not easily accessible. Probably no one in many decades had even known it was there.

Mark always said that water had a sacred element. This water he drank and cooked with and bathed in was a rare thing. He marveled at it. He told me that many of the ancient world's cathedrals and holy places are on spring sites, and that springs had always been considered sacred. I had never heard that before, but I believed him.

Most of the ridges around the area had only two or three year-round springs, Mark told me, but the ranch was lush with seven springs, and he knew the location and strength and course of every one. He knew which were year-round and which ones dried up in the summer. He made sure the spring where he built his house was strong in the summer before he began to build.

He taught me how to search for and recognize a water source. Certain kinds of plants grow near springs, and the ones we called simply water plants were a sure sign of a hidden spring or underground water source. The water plants had big roundish leaves, with little white flowers on spikes. They were tall—well over our heads at the peak of the growing season—and grew in thick patches. Giant ferns, too, were a sign of water, as were cattails, watercress, and forget-me-nots.

I followed Mark all over the ridge, hiking on trails on both the east and west sides, sometimes climbing over logs or wading through overgrown brush as he led me on an intimate tour of this land he knew and loved so much. It was amazing to be discovering all these different places where we lived. The East Canyon, the West Canyon—each had its own unique geography and history, its own character.

Having lived there for two years before I arrived, Mark had grown to know these trails like the back of his hand. Although he had built his house and pond before my arrival, he still loved telling me about it. He told me how he had learned how to dig a pond and build up a dam to hold it. If the mud in the pond was dug out too voraciously, you could dig right into a root or buried log, and the water could wash right down it and come out somewhere else. You had to be careful not to lose the water this way, he said. He was quite proud of it and especially relished the rarity of having his own water system.

He told me that when he put the pond in, there were blue flowers in bloom all around it. A song had come to him as he scooped handfuls of silt and as the water of the spring flowed into the space he had created for it. Later, when we were in his cabin, he played the song for me on his guitar. It was a beautiful classical melody, delicate and timeless. I loved the song and he knew it, and it was one of his favorites to play. The intermingling sounds of his guitar strings sounded like a whole symphony.

It was springtime. The blue flowers were in bloom again. "Those are the ones that inspired the song," Mark told me. The tiny sky-blue blossoms were sprinkled thick across the earth, all around his pond and flowing down the hillside off his porch. En masse, they were like a piece of the sky sitting there. They were one of my favorite wildflowers. "They're called forget-me-nots," I said to him.

9

My wish is to stay always like this,
living quietly, in a corner of nature.
—Claude Monet

Every morning I had been walking barefoot to the Cosmic Kitchen. There were no stickers in the fall. The clay road was just wet enough to feel soft and gooshy to bare feet. As I walked along, I smelled the wood smoke and the aroma of pancakes frying. A deer and two fawns looked up, startled, as I approached. They froze, looking at me, their tails twitching a little. I stopped and we watched each other. Then the spotted fawns turned and took off into the woods to hide. The mother turned her head slightly, as if to appear like she wasn't looking at me, then pranced leisurely away after her young.

Russ, Maggie, and Greg were already there, eating pancakes, passing a joint. They greeted me and encouraged me to put another pancake on the griddle.

Greg dug out an empty plate from the pine needles on the ground. "This is clean," he said. "The cats just knocked it off the shelf last night. Unless it was raccoons. But I'll sterilize it for you." He put the plate into a pot of hot water simmering on the stove.

"We need more pine needles on the floor," Russ said. "Look how matted down this one is."

"How many wheelbarrow loads do we need?" I asked.

"At least six," Greg answered. "For a regular carpet, that covers this whole area. From the stove, under the table, and clear over to those shelves. Yeah, at least six for a regular carpet. Ten for shag."

Maggie's face crinkled into a smile, wrinkling her nose. "Shag?" she laughed.

I looked down at the pine needle carpet. There were bits of twine, avocado peels, and dried carrot tops. There were muddy bare spots and a few little twigs that had blown in. I noticed our feet on the pine needle carpet—Russ's wide and sturdy as if carved out of a solid block of wood, Greg's flat and calloused and cracked like a Neanderthal's, Maggie's arched high like a bird's claw, and mine soft and vulnerable on the soles, a scratch from a berry vine across the top.

Greg gulped at his stiff mug of coffee. "You guys are so lazy!" he said to Maggie and Russ. "I've already hauled two loads of shit to the garden this morning."

"Slow down," Maggie said. "You're so wired on that coffee! I don't see how you can drink it like that. Have another pancake, they're so good!"

Greg ignored her and walked to his wheelbarrow. "I found the most heavenly shit, and there's tons of it! It's back in Buck's pasture, on the other side of the fence. It's so perfect. It's dry enough that you can scoop it right up!"

Russ took a long draw on the joint and then blew it all out, laughing.

We could hear Greg mumbling even as he started to turn and head down the trail. "I shouldn't have even told you, but you probably won't go back there and get any anyway. I used it in the garden, under the peach trees, and two days later they had new growth! Can you believe that?"

"Yeah, sure, I believe that," Russ called after him. "You got it from Buck's pasture?"

Greg paused and set his coffee mug down. "Yeah, there's tons of it! Course he does keep several bulls in that pasture so you have to be careful." He picked up his coffee mug again and walked back to refill it.

"Sounds like you found yourself a whole lot of bullshit, Greg! Go for it." Russ laughed again.

"You should be so lucky," Greg said. "I hope you guys aren't planning on just sitting here all day!"

We could still hear him talking as he maneuvered the wheelbarrow off down the trail. Maggie and Russ took another hit off the joint and handed it to me. Russ stood up and poured more pancake batter on the griddle of the woodstove. The pancakes were dark, rich buckwheat. We piled on homemade butter and pure maple syrup from a five-gallon can. I looked around at the pine needles—the carpet, as they called it. It did indeed perform the job of a carpet. It was about six inches deep and when newly made it looked good, very artistic, clean, fresh, and functional.

"How many wheelbarrow loads did you say it took to carpet this area?" I asked.

"Six," Russ said, and then in unison with Maggie, both of them laughing, "Ten for shag!"

The pine forest at the back of the land was thick with fallen needles. It was easy to scoop them up with both arms and load the wheelbarrow. I was on my fourth trip. I was trying for ten loads.

I continued making trips with the wheelbarrow from the pine forest to the Cosmic Kitchen. I passed the main garden, and the old fire truck that didn't run, and the patch of watercress in the tiny Willow Spring. As I reached the Cosmic Kitchen with each load, I spread out the needles to cover a three- or four-square-foot area several inches deep. I had already swept away any little chunks of wood or avocado peel or carrot top. It was nice to see all that disappear under a fresh, thick layer of pine needles.

After my tenth trip, I sat back and admired my work. The pine needle carpet looked lush and fresh, where before patches of mud had started to show through the old matted layer. I had done it. Ten trips. Shag carpet in the form of pine needles. I smiled and commended myself silently and stuffed some pot I had into the pipe sitting on the stove. Greg and Maggie came up the trail behind me, and when they saw the new carpet they were thrilled.

"Wow!" Greg said. "It's so thick and new, I feel like I'm in suburbia!"

10

> Modern man can't even take a shit in the morning without relying on some government agency!
> —Mike Duncan

There were always visitors trekking to the land. You never knew who would show up. But they were visitors that were connected in some way, not random strangers. Many were previous commune dwellers. There were also friends and family from Middle America who found the lifestyle a little different from what they were used to.

On a warm day, it wouldn't be unusual to see a few people walking around naked or semi-naked. It came to be very natural and commonplace for those of us who lived there. Our visitors would explore the paths and community garden, and marvel at deer that walked by, unstartled by people. Some visitors would be staying with someone who lived there, and others would bring tents or sleep under the stars.

The land itself served as a sort of filter. Since the road in was so rutted and bumpy, it allowed few cars to pass easily. You had to leave your car at some point, at the top of the hill or when you got to the lower gate. At some point you would have to set out on foot, just following paths and dirt roads. None of us drove right up to our cabin, except Bill.

But if visitors made it in and were planning to stay a few days, there was a subject that was difficult but necessary to broach: where to go to "the bathroom," since there were none. Someone would have to tell them where to go and where not to go, and to make sure they had a shovel. It was a big adjustment for some, but it actually made a lot of sense and would quickly start to seem easy and natural.

We did not advocate the disgusting outhouse. NO. We didn't use those. Here, you started with a shovel. You went to a designated spot, private and away from any water source and away from a lot of tree roots, and dug a hole. If you planned to use it a few times, you dug it deeper, about a foot deep. You would leave the shovel there, and if it wasn't the rainy season, you would leave a roll of toilet paper in a container. In spite of our rustic lifestyle, we did use toilet paper. It was simpler to do than you would imagine, and soon it seemed so much more sanitary than a public bathroom. There was no smell, no flies, no weirdness, no porcelain surfaces to collect moisture and germs, no pipes to leak or clog.

For those who lived there, one space would be designated, a clearing, conveniently near the house but not too near. A space that would be rotated as the first hole broke down and was composted and turned into just regular soil. It felt very clean, very natural.

But when a few people's grandmothers came to visit, something had to be done. They were unable to squat. I don't know who it was, but somebody came up with what we called The Throne. It was a strong wooden chair with a tall back to lean against and sturdy armrests. There was a real toilet seat over the hole in the seat of the chair. We dug a deep hole so it could stay in the same place for a few weeks. But it could be picked up and moved anywhere as needed. On one side there was a post with a roll of toilet paper perched on a nail, and on the other side a five-gallon bucket of fresh, loose soil and a scoop. It had one step to climb up, giving it a little extra height. It was placed in a secluded clearing at the end of a smooth, level trail. Many of the older people were reminded of something like they had used as a child. It wasn't that shocking. The air was fresh and the view beautiful. Most of them were well pleased.

11

> Everybody needs beauty as well as bread,
> places to play in and pray in, and give
> strength to body and soul.
> —John Muir

It wasn't long before I tired of my canvas tent and plastic tarp, and I was ready for new and improved housing. This was necessitated to some degree by the approaching winter. Although this was northern California and a temperate climate, I didn't want to be damp or cold. And I needed windows. I wanted to be able to look out around me.

I studied everyone else's cabin and started collecting scraps of wood that were lying around from earlier incarnations of the ranch. I moved in with Mark while I rebuilt. We were together a lot now. I tore off the plastic, took down the stained canvas tent, and tossed out the aluminum tent frame. I cleared the deck until I was standing on the wooden platform, a bare wooden stage in the forest. There was a certain freedom in having no walls. A house with no walls might be quite pleasant, I thought. I sat on the stage, eating dates and tossing the pits off the sides of the stage with theatrical abandon, which I could do since there were no walls. I contemplated my next step.

I invited a few neighbors to advise me on the foundation. The existing foundation was built into the slope of the hill. We decided it just needed bracing. I dragged three bags of concrete down the trail and salvaged some wooden posts about eight inches in diameter. I dug deep holes where the added posts would be, four across one side and two across another. I poured the concrete around each post, pushing it into place with an old shovel. I stepped back to take a broader look while the concrete set. I was told it would take about a day to set up.

The large, lush bay tree that my house would kneel beneath was aromatic, with shiny dark green leaves. I felt like I was getting to know this tree, having slept beneath it for so many nights now. It seemed friendly. I think it liked having me there. It felt like it was protecting me.

As I stood there and studied the situation, I figured the next step was framing. Again, I studied other dwellings that were there, asked some questions, then went back to work with two-by-fours, a hammer, nails, and a saw.

I constructed the first wall. It was about nine feet long and had four two-by-four studs across it. These were nailed top and bottom to another two-by-four. I stood it up and gradually let go. It leaned like an accordion off to one side. I pulled it back up straight again and stood there, not letting go and wondering how I could keep it standing. I had never built anything before in my life. I held it with both feet and one hand and stretched over to the hammer and nails. I got a few really long nails and nailed the bottom two-by-four to the platform. Cautiously, I let go. Again, the wall leaned all the way to one side, and this time it pulled all the nails loose. I was so frustrated I was almost in tears. I sat down, stared at the uncooperative framing, and lit a roach I had in my pocket. I sat there a while, looking at the two-by-four frame that had defeated me. But nothing changed. I had no idea how to make it stand up in place. I picked up my tools and left.

I had to admit I was too easily frustrated. There's always a way if you just don't give up. A few days later I went back to the framing of the walls with new knowledge—diagonals! Mark had enlightened me as to the problem. He showed me how to cut the two-by-four at the correct angle so it attached to the bottom two-by-four securely. I went back to my platform, feeling smug that the wall that had defeated me would now have to cooperate. I picked up where I had left off. I measured where the diagonal two-by-fours should be cut, like Mark had shown me, and got the saw. Then I took that dang accordion wall and nailed the two-by-four diagonally across it, and cautiously let go. It held. I got all the walls framed that day, even on the adjoining porch.

I spent days gathering siding. Everyone used whatever wood they could find, much of which was the remains of previous handmade homes from before Wheeler's was shut down. The homes may have been bulldozed, but the materials were still there to be used again. I dragged or carried the discarded pieces through brush, up and down trails, one or two at a time. It was free. The work made me feel really strong.

Finally I had enough to start nailing the boards onto the frame. Having the siding on made it look like a real house. The boards were old and weathered, different colors, but not rotted. They didn't fit flush against each other. There were lots of cracks. But I kept nailing them up anyway. I'd learned one thing about this type of building—just do whatever works with

the materials you've got, and fix the details later.

By the end of the day, my hammer-gripping arm was sore and cramped. I almost wondered if my arm was permanently damaged, if I'd ever be able to use it again. But there was still siding to be put up and I was feeling so proud of myself, I did a little more. The next day, I finished it, and my arm gradually got back to normal, but stronger.

Mark helped me attach the windows with hinges so they would swing open. That was how his were, and a lot of others too. Part of living here was inviting the outside in, so open windows where the trees and sunlight and sounds came in were common, I found, and desirable. None of the houses on the ranch that I had seen closed the inhabitant off completely from nature. I liked that. We put three windows on one side and two windows on the opposite side. The back wall would be a place to hang things, and the front was open onto the porch. I bought about two dozen slats, one-half inch by two inches, and nailed those onto the siding to cover the cracks between the uneven boards.

There was one small opening on the back wall, too small to attach a window, that was covered with heavy plastic sheeting, secured on the outside. We could never quite seem to get completely away from the incongruous and unecological plastic sheeting as a useful building material. At least half the houses there used it in some small weatherproofing way.

Putting the roof on was a big job. I wanted to be sure it didn't come down on me. I paid Tommy, the best carpenter on the land, twenty dollars to help me. He was glad to get the twenty bucks. We put the rafters up easily in one morning, and the next day we used eight sheets of plywood to cover it. But it wasn't waterproof. I wanted to use real roofing paper like many people had done—like Mark's house and Bill's and the carpenter's—but the rainy season was near and I was running out of money. I was advised to use instead—what else? Plastic! We stretched a heavy sheet of plastic over the roof and anchored it at the sides with some of the leftover slats. The house looked like it was wearing a big shower cap, but it had been a lot of work already and I decided I could live with it.

I had a house. The main room was about nine feet by twelve feet, with lots of windows on two sides. It felt open and inviting. The front of the room adjoined the porch, which was also a little kitchen area. There was a wall halfway across, and the small woodstove was in this little corner between the bed, on the back wall, and the kitchen. I had finished up by constructing a comfortable bed with a foam pad big enough for two people sleeping close together and a storage area underneath. I put in a few shelves and patched up a few holes. I had diagonals everywhere for extra strength and support. Someone had given me a faded pink chair with rockers, and a wooden box that stood on end made a nice little end table. I had found an old wooden screen door that Mark helped me attach to the frame of the porch. None of the houses here had locks. I used a shoestring to tie it closed.

It had taken about six weeks of leisurely but steady hard work, including the time spent collecting building materials. The day came when I could stand back and admire my finished project. I walked inside and looked around at the cabin I had built. The roof had about a dozen bent nails sticking through where I had missed the rafters when I nailed the plywood on. The plastic annoyed me a little. But I looked around and I loved it. To the uninitiated, the house would appear to be a crooked shack, made up of mismatched materials and studded with bent nails and a roof wearing a shower cap. But I saw it the way I knew it would be. In my eyes, there were prisms hanging in the windows, beautiful pictures tacked up on the walls, open windows revealing fir trees and wild lilac and blue sky, and a warm fire in the woodstove. I was pleased. It was the first, the only, thing I had ever built.

Like Thoreau at Walden, only a little more loosely, I could estimate the cost of the building materials for my house: twenty-five two-by-fours, twelve that I salvaged and thirteen I bought for $.79 each; ten sheets of plywood, enough for the roof and the bed, at $4 each; two dozen slats, three boxes of nails, and some stovepipe, for less than $10. Mark gave me a wood stove he wasn't using, and Ambriel gave me the end of a roll of heavy plastic sheeting she didn't need. All of the siding, the windows, and the posts for the foundation were free, salvaged. The grand total came to $60.27. I took it out of my savings that I'd been living on, from what I had earned working before I left Oregon. But I had money left, and I had a house.

Years later I look back on that house and marvel. It certainly was no pinnacle of construction in today's terms, but in the years I lived there, it sheltered me through some of the worst storms recorded in a hundred years. My first winter there held the record for the heaviest winds recorded in the past century. All over the county, trees fell. At least two hundred Douglas-firs, fifty to eighty feet tall and as many years old, fell in our area of the county. But not a branch hit my house.

Another winter boasted some of the heaviest rainfall ever recorded in the area. I remember how hard and continuously it rained, all day and on into the night, and then all through the night into the next morning. The ground turned into slick, wet clay, and whole hillsides slid away, trees, rocks, and all. An overflowing river crashed right over the road into town, ripping a gaping hole in the asphalt. But my house stood firm. The sheets of water rushing down the hill toward my house formed detours and funneled away on either side. The big old bay tree on whose roots the house was planted gripped the earth and kept it from washing away.

We were warm and cozy in the midst of those storms. Sitting barefoot and comfortable, often with the hinged windows flung open and the raindrops pounding the roof, we were kept warm by the woodstove. We even made a tape during that storm, on a little battery-operated cassette recorder. Mark was sitting on the bed playing his guitar and singing and the tape caught the background sounds of the pattering rain outside. I still have that tape. I still listen to it.

But those wild winters passed and we survived just fine, without indoor plumbing, electricity, or building code certified studs in the walls eighteen inches apart.

12

*I want to live free in nature,
the way one lives in cowboy movies.*
—Mrs. Mandik of Yugoslavia

I tore out of the newspaper, the San Francisco Chronicle, a story about the Mandiks in Yugoslavia, who had taken their children out of school, sold their house and car, and moved into the woods to live life simply. They were considered quite eccentric, enough to have made international news. It was 1979. As I read about them, it made perfect sense to me. I knew exactly what she meant about the cowboy movies. That was just her point of reference—she was talking about the freedom and autonomy of living away from modern society, living close to nature.

There was more to it than just growing your own food and not having a regular job. There was a lawlessness to it that invited personal freedom. It expanded your sense of living. Our term *voluntary simplicity* was full of meaning that went beyond basic back-to-the-land living. Mrs. Mandik confirmed for me in personal terms that this was a universal urge, the desire for something different, something more than our traditional modern world can provide. Something real and natural.

Voluntary primitivism, another way to describe it, was no longer an experimental philosophy, no longer a strange and uncharted lifestyle. To us, it had become standard, our way of life. Although it was illegal to build simple handmade shelters without plumbing or electricity, against all building codes and standard practices, people all over the country were doing it anyway, and quite successfully. We learned from each other, and we learned from experience. It was surprising to realize how little money you actually need when you have free access to land and water.

I tacked the newspaper clipping about the Mandiks onto the two-by-four post next to my sitting chair, next to a watercolor painting I had done. It was tacked up, too. No frame. Simple. I finished reading the newspaper, set it aside to start a fire with in the woodstove later on, and went outside to wash up.

The heavy rains and winter storms were over. We could feel it in the way the sun shone, even though it was still cold. The earliest spring plants were already three inches high, and growing fast. The miner's lettuce was thick in patches around the springs and tucked into shady clusters under trees. I had learned where all the best spots were to find them. The leaves of miner's lettuce start out teardrop shaped and grow fuller and rounder until the leaf reaches all the way around and becomes a round leaf with the stem sticking through the middle. That's when it's at its best, before the tiny white flower sprouts out of the middle, but they're still tasty and edible even after flowering. We picked them nearly every day for a salad. We were starting to plant lettuce and peas in the garden, but the

Swiss chard and lemon sorrel that grew most of the year were already big enough to harvest. The three greens together made a tasty, hearty salad with a light dressing of olive oil, lemon or vinegar, and tamari. We could easily eat a large serving bowl of salad for dinner, and we often did.

    I had never felt as good as these days when I ate mostly rice, beans, and salad. I was outside most of the time, and worked in the garden, and hiked the trails to and from our homes, the garden, the canyons, and up to the front gate where I parked Betsy. I ate huge portions of rice, beans, and salad, and I was stronger than I had ever been before. I felt relaxed and had put on more muscle, partly also due to cutting firewood. I saw a kind side of human nature, where the less you have, the more you share, and the more you appreciate what you do have. We shared meals and traded food we bought in town. We all had a few sources of money, from occasional jobs in the community or selling crafts, or in Mark's case, playing music. We didn't need much. But not everyone had money. So we shared and traded, and together, we got by.

13

Just living is not enough. One must have
sunshine, freedom, and a little flower.
—Hans Christian Andersen

I was eagerly looking forward to my first May Day on the ranch. The celebration had been held every year for years before I was there, and I was excited.

When I woke that morning, there was a feeling as if fairies had been at work in the night. Something magical was in the air. Before I even had my coffee, I walked barefoot to the open field where the celebration would be. Someone had hung ribbons and bells from the trees to guide visitors down the road to the big event. The rainbow-colored streamers were already attached to the maypole, and a wreath of pink, purple, white, and red flowers encircled the top.

Past the garden, the fire for the sauna rocks

was already burning, and the rocks were beginning to heat up. One by one, scattered chimneys all across the ridgetop began to smoke, coffee and herb tea began to brew, and eggs were frying. Axes rang out, splitting kindling, and voices called out and answered. From deep in the canyon, I heard a drum, then another, and the sound of hoots and laughter. Guests from the city came to May Day every year, arriving the night before, hiking in, and sleeping outside. We had been planning this for weeks. The day before, Russ and Maggie and I had spent all day grinding soybeans and brewing soy milk sweetened with maple syrup. We had made four gallons. We had baked six pies—blueberry and apple and lemon tofu cheesecake. We had kept the stove in the Cosmic Kitchen burning long after the stars came out.

All morning, a parade of guests trekked down the road to the May Day field. They came in groups, or alone, couples, old people, young people, hippies in headbands and faded jeans and long flowered skirts, city people looking hip and fashionable, the grown-up children of local farmers in denim and plaid shirts and cowboy boots.

As the crowd swelled, so did the music. Mark had joined the group of musicians and sat with his guitar, jamming with Cliff, Nathan, Moses, Delia, and various guests with drums, guitars, harmonicas, flutes, maracas, and a dulcimer. Ramon arrived with his accordion. Singers joined in, and dancers, smiling and joyful. We had put several large tables out to hold the feast, and they began to fill with baskets of raspberries and nectarines, pots of rice and beans, homemade tortillas, wild green salads with freshly picked herbs and edible flowers. There were the four gallons of soy milk, and buckets of lemonade, and the pies, bowls of popcorn, and vases of lilacs, roses, and hollyhocks. There were chocolate cakes, carrot cakes, cornbread, lasagna, enchiladas, and salsa. Kegs of beer and bottles of wine filled a bathtub full of ice.

The earliest guests, the old-timers, knew to gather at the sauna. There was always a group sauna on Sundays and on special occasions. On May Day, many of the guests who had spent the night started their day here. As the rocks began to glow in the fire, clothes were shed, and someone would grab the pitchfork and lift the rocks into the center pit of the canvas dome. Three large rocks and two or three small ones made a nice long, hot sauna. Long enough to get out twice and plunge into a tub of cold water or cool down with the water from the hose. The steam rising from the rocks would warm you to the bone once again when you went back in. It was a bonding ritual, as well as a healthy one.

While the sauna baked, the crowd mingled around the field, around the maypole and the musicians and the tables laden with food, meeting old friends and making new ones. By late afternoon, it would be time to start the maypole dance. Whoever wanted to grabbed a streamer, some eager like the kids, and first-time guests who needed to be coaxed. Age was not a factor—it was open to all. The musicians strolled closer and began to play, and the dance began. Some walked, some twirled or danced, and holding the streamers wound in and around each other, half going one direction and the other half going the opposite.

It was a fun, free-form, somewhat disorganized ritual, but somehow the streamers wound around the pole, blue crossing pink, crossing yellow and green, and orange and red, weaving in and out and crossing around and down the pole. This was an ancient tradition to celebrate spring, revived in modern times. When the last streamer was finally wound tightly around the bottom of the pole, a cheer went up. The May Pole stood

completed, a majestic monolith with its flowered crown, a tribute to another beautiful celebration.

The party continued till nightfall, the rhythmic drums beating from all over the hills and the guests dividing eventually into small groups crammed into individual homes hidden in the woods or circling the still-burning fire of the sauna. Then the city people went back to the city, friends went home, and raccoons feasted on the leftovers in the field that night.

Wild Things

If I only had to talk to trees,
I could breathe easy.
But my face plays the mystery movie
while my heart's never at home.

Talk to me of castles in the sky
now that I understand.
But I'm afraid I'll never make it
with the lunchbox crowd.

I eat at home,
greens and wild things.
I eat wild things from the canyon
(Jane eats wild boar)
and I really mean to be here.

But when the full moon glows so bright
and mourns so sweetly,
what else can I do?
A tree house, a white horse, a prism,
one eye green, one eye blue.

If I only had to talk to stars,
now that I could do.

14

Lives are like songs. They have beginnings,
middles, and ends. God bless the musicians
of the world. The makers of music.
The singers of song.
—Carol Cronin (Mark's sister)

The first thing I remember
is a beautiful song
in a world full of singing.

And it makes me wonder,
mmm hmmmm,
it makes me wonder.

When I first heard Mark sing this song, I wondered if he really did come into the world this way, to the sound of a beautiful song. I bet he did. I bet a beautiful song was his first memory of life. What a beautiful concept, to come into the world to the sounds of some celestial otherworldly music. The sound of birth from the other side of the veil, singing us into this life.

Whenever Mark saw how tuned in I was to his songs, he just glowed. It was wonderful to be tapped into the same wavelength. Maybe that's what plucks the strings of love. It certainly was a part of it. I always marveled at the rhythm and melodies he could be weaving together all at one time. His fingers on the strings sounded like more than what just one person and one instrument could produce.

If I could relive any one moment of my life over and over, it would be one of these moments, when we were sitting in his cabin, or mine, and he was playing his beautiful original music, one song after another. Time would stand still and that moment would live in eternity.

15

> Flowers always make people better,
> happier, and more helpful: they are sunshine, food,
> and medicine for the soul.
> —Luther Burbank

I had not been off the land in over a month, and even then it was only to pick up my mail at the post office. The garden was flourishing, and I had everything I needed. I had friends and neighbors within walking distance, fresh air, fresh water, warm days and cool nights. I had books to read and music to listen to.

In summer, everything was ripe. All of the work in spring, all the planting, watering, weeding, and waiting, had come to fruition. There were only seven or eight of us who worked in the garden, some more than others, but the garden produced more than enough. We had three different kinds of tomatoes and five different kinds of peppers. In raised beds, we had green beans, lima beans, fava beans, and purple-and-white-spotted Aztec beans. We grew cucumbers and every color of onion—red, yellow, and white. We grew squash and carrots and beets. The raspberries, which had been planted years ago, ran more than halfway around the two-acre garden. We had strawberries and a red peach tree, and we even planted a mulberry tree. We got eight mulberries that first year.

There were fifteen long rows of corn. Bill had tilled that section of the garden with his tractor. There's something ancient about corn, and when you walk between the rows, you hear the unique rustle of cornstalks. Never is corn so sweet and juicy as when you pick it and eat it raw, while you're standing right there in the cornfield, with the blue sky above and the cornstalks singing all around you.

The flowers were a maze of color and attracted hummingbirds and butterflies. Hollyhocks in deep red and pale peach. Red roses and yellow roses and pink cosmos. Snapdragons, deep blue bachelor buttons, bright orange poppies and calendula, and pale blue love-in-a-mist. The cats lazed in patches of catnip on hot afternoons, nonchalant about the gophers they were supposed to catch.

I had gotten used to working in the garden and coming home with a basket of fresh carrots, beets, beans, and tomatoes. I had planted some more things in the little garden by my house, too, not vegetables but flowers and herbs. It was much shadier than the main garden that we all shared. I had planted sage, thyme, oregano, and nasturtiums, edible flowers that were red, gold, and orange. The chard did pretty well here, too. Chard would grow just about anywhere. I planted some bright red geraniums and they got huge, unexpectedly for the amount of sunlight they got. They were almost three feet tall, and thick with dozens of deep red blossoms.

Most people think plants just stand around and don't do anything, but they are constantly interacting with their environment. Their world is alive with flying insects of all kinds, bees, dragonflies, and spiders climbing around and spinning webs. They take in oxygen and breathe out carbon dioxide, and are affected by air currents, airborne pollen, deer, gophers, cows, birds, raindrops, fog, mist, sunbeams, and people, like me. Time passes for them and they experience seasons, putting down roots, blossoming, and going to seed.

    I felt like I knew them, like I knew the big bay tree that we lived by. The garden had become so overgrown that I had to bend down and squeeze in because the jasmine had spread across the chicken wire gate. I stretched out on the garden platform, where I had made myself a bed, and drifted off. The red geraniums were dazzling, even through half-closed eyes, and the overgrown jasmine vine filled me with its perfume. I loved being here, in this very spot.

Retreat into the Garden

I crawl through the secret tunnel.
Overhanging jasmine hides my escape
and ripe raspberries dangle before my lips.
I come out into the sun.
The pathway stretches before me up to the altar.
I breathe,
I see color,
green and vibrant red,
attracting hummingbirds.
A fast whirr of wings flying past my ears,
bits of yellow and purple and white
on a jungle tapestry of green.
I breathe the tangled plants
and they breathe me.
The sun gets warmer, then hot,
and when it gets too hot,
even though my head is protected with a straw hat,
I run for the shade,
escaping out the way I came in,
through the jasmine.

16

> Life is this simple. We are living in a world
> that is absolutely transparent and God is
> shining through it all the time. God is
> manifest everywhere, in everything, in people
> and in things, in nature and in events.
> It becomes very obvious that God is every-
> where and in everything and we cannot be
> without God. It's simply impossible.
> —Thomas Merton

As summer turned into fall, and knowing winter would follow soon after, I quickly learned which of the native trees were best for firewood. We cut only the dead trees and branches. We didn't need a lot of firewood in this relatively temperate climate, especially with just a small space to heat. I spent several long afternoons foraging in the woods below my house and amassed a pretty good pile of ceanothus branches. Competing with the bigger firs and oaks, these trees rarely got bigger than ten inches in diameter in the thick of the woods. They were easy to cut with my new bow saw.

I wore my boots when getting wood, and just jeans and a long-sleeved shirt. It was fun, looking for just the right pieces to cut, being alone in the woods, listening to the birds chirping, listening to my neighbors in the distance talking or laughing. I cut the ceanothus branches into sizes that were easy to carry back up, where I would cut them smaller to fit into the woodstove. The crackly dry coyote bushes snapped easily into small pieces of kindling and caught fire easily. I was always able to get a good stack of these without even using the saw. The best find, especially in wet weather, was the charred branches of old fir trees left from when a fire had seared the area about fifty years earlier. No matter how wet the charcoaled bark was, the inside was dry, and they burned hot and gave off more heat than other woods, and lasted longer. The straight grain made these pieces so easy to cut, they nearly popped apart at the first touch of the ax.

I carried the pieces up the hill and sawed or chopped the bigger pieces until I had accumulated a nice pile of kindling and bigger pieces. Some I stacked in the cabin, within easy reach of the stove, and the rest I stacked in a little lean-to by the side of the house that was covered with a sheet of plastic. I estimated that it would be enough to last three or four weeks before I'd need to cut more. It felt good to cut my own firewood. My arms, back, and shoulders felt stronger than they'd ever been.

But it was enough for one day. I had worked alone all afternoon and was starting to crave human contact. I set my boots and the ax inside the porch. I liked seeing the new stack of firewood lined up in varying sizes, the kindling on one side and the bigger pieces on the other, since I had used my last few pieces of firewood earlier that morning to heat water on the stove for my shower. One pot of almost-boiling water poured into a bucket filled halfway with cold water was enough to provide almost a five-gallon bucket of water at the perfect temperature. There had been a short rain this morning just before dawn, and even though it was cool, it wasn't too cold to stand naked and ladle the warm water over me as I stood outside the little garden by my house. It was a ritual I had grown to love.

I pulled on a vinyl raincoat and arranged a lambswool hat over my long hair, and started up the trail. The sky was gray and moody. Clouds drifted in and then went on by, almost as if the sky couldn't decide whether to storm or not. I felt a few raindrops on my face. I heard the sound of someone chopping wood. As I reached the top of my trail, I heard children laughing and saw Victor and Skye, both six years old, hurrying along the road toward me.

"We caught a frog!" called Skye, "Look! We caught a frog!" Skye held the frog carefully in both hands and walked cautiously as Victor bounced along at his side, bumping into him.

"Let me hold him!" Victor cried. "Let me touch him!"

The two boys stopped as Skye held the frog toward me, and Victor grimaced a smile and ran his fingers along the slimy green back of the frog.

"We caught a frog!" Skye announced again proudly.

"That's a big frog!" I said, touching its webbed feet. "Did you find it by the pond?"

"Yeah," Victor answered. "We been trying to catch this frog for three days!"

"But we're not gonna keep him," Skye smiled. "We're gonna take him back to the pond and let him go. We just wanted to catch him, huh Victor?"

"Yeah," Victor agreed, "so let me hold him!"

"Okay, here," Skye said, passing the treasured frog to Victor. "Ya got him, Victor? Ya got him? Watch it, he's trying to get loose! Hold him but don't squish him!" They were both giggling.

Victor started to laugh and the frog continued to squirm.

"He's slippery!" Victor squealed. "He's getting loose!" Suddenly the frog wiggled free and with one slimy bounce, landed at least five feet away in the grass, and then with three more quick leaps he was gone down the hill.

"Come on, Skye!" Victor yelled. "Let's go find him."

"Nah. We were gonna let him go anyway. Might as well just let him go," Skye answered. "Let's go to Bob's. Ya want to?"

"Sure," said Victor. "I bet he has some Hershey bars or Oreos. He always does."

"Yeah," Skye said, "I thought about that."

I watched them as they headed off together down the dirt road, barefoot, best friends, picking up pinecones and seeing who could throw the farthest.

"See ya, Joy!" they called out.

"Okay, nice seein' ya!" I called back.

What a world for a child to grow up in, I thought. Since birth, these two boys had had a few hundred acres or more of meadows and forests and friends to explore. Their mothers knew where they were and kept an eye on them, and they were under loose supervision for their own safety. But within certain parameters, they had an amazing amount of independence and freedom. They were confident and self-reliant.

Now they were walking about two-thirds of a mile down a dirt road where the only inhabitants along the way were friends, and they were as familiar with the lay of the land as with their own house. Bob kept a play area for them by the library in the pine trees, filled with plastic army men, plastic farm animals, and toy dinosaurs. There were Legos, building blocks, various odd-sized pieces of wood, and small empty cardboard boxes, and apparently Hershey bars and Oreos.

17

The goal of life is to make your heartbeat
match the beat of the universe, to match
your nature with Nature.
—Joseph Campbell

Mark had a new vehicle—Betsy. I was feeling so entranced with the land that I felt free to let go of her. I just wanted to be there. If I needed to go somewhere, Mark or Bill, or one of the other two people with trucks, could take me. I felt a little bit bad about letting her go, but I was falling so in love with this place that I didn't want to go anywhere else. Mark hadn't had a vehicle in a couple years. He was ready to be more mobile. So he gave me four hundred dollars as a down payment, and we headed into town. There was nothing I needed. I just wanted to hang out with him. He didn't want me to sign over the title, not just yet.

Mark and Betsy had an instant connection.

He loved being behind the wheel again, and especially in something that fit in so well at the ranch. He was smiling as he took the first drive after I relinquished the keys to him, even though he had driven her before. Betsy rumbled up the dirt road like the workhorse she was, bouncing and climbing up to the main road. Mark was elated with his new mobility.

Any day now, he was expecting his friends Ted and Diane from Long Beach to visit. Two of his musician friends from L.A. had just left. They had somehow made it down to the lower gate and asked someone how to find Mark. We laughed about it now as we were driving along in Betsy, into Occidental, and remembering how lost and helpless they were in the woods. Whoever had told them to head down the hill near the beginning of Mark's trail and then left them there must have gotten a kick out of it. They wouldn't have been lost for long. They weren't even very far from the road, but they were in a wooded area and all they could see was trees. Mark was nearby, heard them yelling, and came to their aid. Somehow we got a kick out of seeing city people so clueless about the woods.

"I was just washing up, and I hear these voices coming from up the hill," Mark laughed, remembering, "and I went up and there they were, way off course and ducked down under some branches. Yelling for me—'Mark! Help!'" he laughed, imitating their cries.

"They looked very, well, overdressed for the woods," I smiled. "And their hair looked perfect!" I had seen them on the road, and they were in some kind of shiny-looking bright pants, and dressy jackets, and boots that were not made for trails. On a stage in a big city, they would have looked great. Surrounded by trees and brush and fallen logs, looking lost and bewildered, they looked hilariously out of place.

"They came straight from the studio," Mark said. "They said they didn't sleep all night, they just drove up here after recording. God, I can't believe they made it all the way down the hill!"

"What did they think of the ranch?" I asked.

"Oh, they didn't even comprehend it! They think I'm crazy to be out here. Gary just put money down on a house in Laguna, and Rick's buying a Ferrari—those guys are in debt up to their eyeballs, and they don't even care. It's just the norm in that world. They're recording, and working constantly to pay for it. But they're not writing. That's what I like about this place. I'm writing music all the time!

"They tried to talk me into going back to L.A. with them. They didn't even spend the night. I walked them back up the hill so they could get a room in town. They never would have made it out on their own!" Mark shook his head. "But Ted and Diane are different. They've been here once before and they love it. They're cool. You'll like them. Ted and I go way back—we went to high school together."

Ted and Diane made it down the road a few days later. David had seen them at the front gate and pointed them toward the trail to my place, much easier to find than Mark's. I had picked wild miner's lettuce, lemon sorrel, and watercress for a salad. We had been having these wild-picked salads almost every night, and they were delicious. We had some brown rice and black beans, and potatoes from the garden, simmering in butter and herbs on the woodstove.

Mark had asked me earlier that day to invite David to join us for dinner if I saw him. I walked down the trail to his platform. David had just a wooden platform for his sleeping bag, and a small covered basket to keep his things. He wasn't there. I tried to figure out how to leave him a message. No paper or pen handy. Hmmm. I noticed a lot of pinecones on the ground. I gathered some up and laid them out to spell S-A-L-A-D and then formed an arrow with pinecones pointing to my house. David loved our wild greens salads. I hoped he would figure it out.

Later that morning, before our guests arrived, we realized we were short on silverware. We only had two spoons and two forks. So it seemed a miracle that while digging potatoes in the garden, I unearthed three forks and a spoon, just what we needed for dinner that night. The earth does provide!

It was not unusual to find silverware in the garden. Bill collected the discarded food and table scraps from the local vegetarian restaurant, the Blue Heron Inn, and fed it to the hungry red worms in the worm bin. Silverware that was mistakenly discarded now and then worked its way through the worm bins and into the soil as the composted garbage was made into soil-enriching worm castings, then dug in and hoed. It was eventually found by someone, like now.

When Ted and Diane hooted at the top of the trail to signal their arrival, we hooted back. The silverware had been washed with dish soap and rinsed thoroughly at the outdoor faucet, and was simmering in a pan of boiling water. By the time it was ready for use, it would be thoroughly sterilized.

Ted and Diane loved being here. They loved having a rustic retreat from city life. They got it. Among the hugs and smiles and laughter, Ted opened a bottle of wine. We did have enough cups. As he poured the wine and Mark rolled a joint, we heard David coming down the trail. He was chuckling.

"You saw my note!" I said to him. "I guess you knew what it meant!"

David couldn't stop smiling. "Of course!" he said. And we poured another cup of wine.

18

We must fix our eyes not on what is seen, but what is unseen. For what is seen is temporary, but what is unseen is eternal.
—2 Corinthians 4:18

Mark loved being a tour guide for me. When we were out and about, driving Betsy, he told me stories about the local history of the area. We both loved hearing about Morningstar. I asked Mark to take me there. I wanted to see the place. So one day we decided to visit Morningstar, ten years after it had been shut down. No one had lived there all that time. I was excited.

Morningstar had closer neighbors than the ranch. The ranch was much more isolated, due to the location and the lay of the land. Just outside of Occidental, we drove in on the long curving driveway, parked Betsy, and got out to look around. No one was living there at the time. It was just the way I had seen it in the pictures.

As we walked along, we imagined how it must have been.

And then we met a woman who had come back. She had lived at Morningstar at the height of its notoriety and activity, and now she lived in L.A. and had brought her teenage son here to see the place that had changed her life. Tears were streaming down her face as she looked around, remembering, and she told us, "We didn't know anything about living like that. We learned." Morningstar was a place she would never forget. Her son had grown up in the city, and he looked around at the unfamiliar landscape and the orchard and meadows as his mother looked back in time.

"There's a persimmon tree down that trail," she reminisced. "Our house was right over there, at the edge of the meadow. We built it ourselves and it was beautiful. It was a little shack, octagon-shaped, and it was beautiful." She wanted her son to see what she saw.

"You were conceived and born here," she told him. And she told him how it all ended. That the court decreed that God could not own land, because He could not walk into court and sign His name. Because of that ruling, and the numerous building code and health code violations, Morningstar was shut down. The houses were demolished by the county bulldozer, and everyone was either run off the property or arrested for being there.

Mark and I listened intently as she talked about her memories of living at Morningstar. It wasn't all good. There were some serious conflicts and issues with drugs and cops and the health department and some people who didn't have good intentions for being there. But most of it was good and fascinating. She was one of the good ones who came there. She wanted her son, and us, to know that she would never forget that place and that experience. She was so moved just being there again, and hearing her tell about it, so were we.

"There were all kinds of people who came," she said. "Old, young, rich, poor. There were bikers, and artists and musicians, people that were outcasts, or some who were just wanting to escape a mundane world of work. A lot of people who came didn't even know where they were headed, but they knew what they wanted to leave behind."

I thought about her and the things she told us for weeks afterward. It was almost like meeting your own ancestors. The way I lived now was in direct correlation to the experience she had had at Morningstar.

I had been here long enough now to know the land really well. I knew the location of all the wild plants I wanted to gather today and had been looking forward to this time I'd set aside for that purpose.

The nettles were still young and not tough yet. We'd had them several times lately in soup with garlic and potatoes from the garden. Eating nettles made me feel like Popeye with his spinach. I put heavy gloves and scissors in a paper bag so I could pick them without getting stung. The heart-shaped leaves of the nettle were notorious for the bee-sting-like pain they could inflict if they touched your bare skin. I had learned how to identify nettles and avoid touching them, but every so often while picking them, even with gloves, or sometimes just walking by, the innocent-appearing plant would reach out and sting. When cooked, the leaves were harmless. There was no sting in them then. They were full of vitamin B12 and iron, and tasted kind of smoky and green.

I had seen mugwort and mullein growing at the bottom of the East Canyon. I decided I would start there. I was going to dry them, and I wanted to pick the nettles and the salad greens last so they would still be fresh when I got back to make dinner. I didn't like the taste of either mugwort or mullein, but both had medicinal purposes and it was good to have them on hand. The silvery gray mullein leaves were as soft as a rabbit's ears. I liked them to use as a tea that was soothing to the throat and lungs.

Mugwort was supposed to be good for circulation and digestion, and it was said to enable you to see the future. I wasn't expecting that to happen, but it would be good in tea blended with more flavorful herbs, and sometimes I just liked to keep it in a vase. It was pretty.

The yerba buena that grew everywhere had a sweeter, smoky, mint taste that flavored any herb blend, and I really liked the taste of it. The small oval leaves, lined up symmetrically along the stem, grew in several places I had seen, so I would pick some of it when I saw a really good thick patch.

I had grown familiar with the trail to the East Canyon. Even when I was walking leisurely and barefoot, it took me only about twenty-five minutes to reach the bottom. It was a beautiful, easy hike that wound down through the same stand of redwoods that I could see the tops of from Mark's house. It was quiet and peaceful walking down. When I reached the bottom, I saw that the creek was fairly low. The rocky streambed near the end of the trail was where I had seen mugwort and mullein growing. I nibbled on some watercress that was growing in a little tributary. It was hot and peppery. This patch was younger than the patch by the Willow Spring. I made a mental note that this patch would still be good when the other patch up the hill started to flower.

The pale blue forget-me-nots were in bloom and filled a whole area under the white-barked alders like a little patch of sky sitting on the ground. I waded in the creek a ways. Tiny fish scattered away from my steps. I lay on a large flat rock for a while, feeling the warmth of the sun and the stillness

and incredible privacy, and thought as I often still did how incredible it was to be sitting here in this beautiful place, alone and safe and free, in paradise. Picking the herbs I had come for and putting them in the basket I had brought, I looked back at the alluring creek, hesitant to go. Sometimes I stayed longer when I came down here, but today there was more I wanted to do, so I decided reluctantly to head back up the trail, knowing the amazing fact that I could come back anytime I wanted to.

When I reached the top of the trail, I went by the Willow Spring and picked some watercress, and then I stopped by the main garden and picked some Swiss chard, Russian tarragon, a few onions, and a handful of spinach. From there I went on down the dirt road and picked dandelion greens, mallows, sorrel, and plantains growing in patches off to the sides of the road. I found a patch of fiddlehead ferns with the curled tips that had a nutlike flavor, and I picked some of those. There was a patch of miner's lettuce just below my house, so I would pick that after I got back.

Seeing the heavy gloves in the bottom of the basket that I had covered with greens, I realized I had forgotten the nettles. I knew where a patch of them grew behind the garden, and I was not far past it. I set the basket of greens in a tree, took the paper bag and gloves, and went back to get the nettles. I picked nine stems. Later I would hold them with the gloves and use the scissors to cut the leaves off directly into a pan.

I went back and got the basket from the tree, and walked toward home. I had accumulated a lot of greens and herbs in my pleasant morning hike, more than enough for Mark and me. I hoped I would encounter somebody, whoever was walking on the road, and whoever it turned out to be, I would invite them to join us for dinner.

19

> If civilization is to survive, we must
> cultivate the science of human
> relationships—the ability of all peoples,
> of all kinds, to live together,
> in the same world at peace.
> —Franklin D. Roosevelt

Mark had a tab at Rocco's Bar and Grill. It was a gas station, too, and Mark was a regular there. We had both had a lot of quiet time on the ranch lately, and when Mark said he was going into town and asked me to go along, I decided to go. Mark had given me another four hundred dollars for Betsy. He still didn't want to put his name on the title. It didn't matter. We were together practically all the time now. I used to joke with him that it was the best car deal I'd ever made. I sold the car but still had both the car and the driver.

Rocco and his pretty Italian wife, Maria,

both loved Mark. They knew most of the locals, but they treated Mark almost like a son. "Hey, Marco!" Rocco would say with a smile whenever Mark would roll in, and Maria, too, was always glad to see him. She would get him a Budweiser as soon as he sat down. "You want a burg today?" Rocco would say. He always dropped the -er. "You want a burg?" Rocco's burgers were well known in the area. He raised his own grass-fed beef, and Maria made a salsa that they served with the burgers. That was what made the restaurant unique.

I was a vegetarian, but it didn't seem right in this environment, not at Rocco's. At first I stuck with just Maria's potato salad with her homemade salsa on it and a Coke. But those burgs looked really good, and when I finally tried one, I was hooked. I may have still been a vegetarian at heart, but not when I was at Rocco's with Mark.

It was a small place on a semi-main road surrounded by farms and fields. The town, what there was of it, was called Freestone, like in freestone peaches. This was Luther Burbank's old stomping grounds. He probably developed the freestone peach right there. I read Luther Burbank's biography once. It said he developed spineless cactuses by talking to them and reassuring them they would be protected and no longer needed spines. He must have developed the freestone peaches by teaching the fruit to let go of their pits more freely. Luther Burbank was amazing. *The Autobiography of a Yogi*, a popular book in the counterculture, was dedicated to Luther Burbank.

We talked about all these things driving down the country roads in Betsy on our way to Rocco's, about all the things that had gone on there, like Morningstar and Wheeler's, and Luther Burbank, and the proposed nuclear plant, and the logging, the livestock ranches, and the growth of the counterculture movement of the times. We talked about how exciting it all was.

Mark was a great tour guide. He pointed out protected

groves of redwood trees as we passed by and told me their story, and told me about the proposed nuclear plant and how it had been shut down before it was finished, and showed me the exact spot where it was going to be. He knew a lot of the locals who had told him about the history and character of the place, and about the changes the land itself had been through. I was much quieter and slower to get to know people than Mark was, but when I was with him it was easier to be a part of things. He took me on a regular route through the community, and introduced me to the farmers, the sheep ranchers, the fishermen, the bar owners, and the local politicians. And he introduced me to Rocco and Maria. We spent many fun times with them, chatting and laughing and enjoying burgs and beer.

It was the usual crowd at Rocco's that day. Claude Bell was sitting at the bar sobbing into his beer and getting carried away with the tearjerker song on the radio.

"She called me Punkin'," he sang to Maria, "and died in my arms . . ."

Claude's face was round and red, his eyes squinty and wet. He tipped the beer bottle to his mouth and took a crooked swig. Most of the sloshy brew found its way into his mouth, and the last bit dribbled down the side of his chin. He tipped his head back a little, opened his mouth crooked like a comedic vaudeville star, and sang again, "She called me Punkin' and died in my arms." He took another swig and then spoke intently to the bottle, "I loved my wife, you know, and she died in my arms."

Maria had had enough of Claude. She knew how to handle all of her regular customers. "Nobody wanna heara your problem," she said to him, shaking her head and sweeping her hand back at him as she walked away.

"His wife didn't die," she said to another customer sitting at the opposite end of the bar. The woman looked concerned. Maria leaned on the bar to talk to her. "He's just drunk. She was in here this afternoon. I just talked to her. He shouldn't be driving. She's going to pick him up."

An old ranch hand, Bernie Jordan, smiled down the bar at Claude and nodded his head a little, meaning to reassure him and pretend not to notice how drunk he was. Bernie was seventy-six and had worked on the same two ranches for more than forty years, except for a few years during World War II when he had served in the Army and was stationed in France. He did the same work he had done for decades, and as the years went by he just kept doing it and was almost as strong and durable as a man half his age. Mark and I had enjoyed hearing his stories when he was in the mood to tell them.

Rocco had three hamburgers on the grill. He always cooked the burgers himself. "That's the only way you can get them perfect," he said. They were the best in the area—that was undisputed. Sometimes if someone would ask Rocco for change for the telephone, he would reach into the cash drawer without looking and in a flash draw out the exact number of quarters, dimes, and nickels asked for and then swing around and bang the cash register drawer closed with his hip.

Bart was at his usual spot that day down at the end of the bar, the best position to see the TV. He had been keeping an eye on the TV since he'd gotten there. Today Bart was a celebrity. He clutched his beer and kept an eye on the TV, and mumbled to whoever would listen. He had a new job, and he wanted to tell somebody about it. It was just temporary, but then, all of Bart's jobs were temporary. Somehow he was able to keep coming up with them. He could cook, paint houses, and chop firewood. He fixed minor car problems and repaired fencing. He could always find something between times of hanging out at Rocco's, running up his bill. Rocco gave credit to all his friends. He knew they would always pay. Bart tried to run up his bill as high as possible before getting a job.

Suddenly something on the TV caught Bart's attention.

"Hey Claude," Bart called into Claude's dramatic and tearful reverie. "Hey Claude, watch what's coming up next." Bart motioned toward the TV. "I'm gonna be on TV!"

"Oh, come on," Maria said, curious and slightly impressed. "Whaddya mean you're gonna be on TV?" She looked at Mark and me with doubt about Bart's claim on her face.

"It's news to me!" Mark shrugged.

"Just watch," Bart said proudly, taking a Bogart-like drag of his cigarette. "Channel Two. They filmed me. Filmed me judging this contest in Guerneville."

Bernie was happy for Bart and grinned, his teeth white against his deeply tanned face. "You really gonna be on TV? That's great! Good for you!" Bernie bought everybody a round. Maria filled the glasses.

"Here it is!" Bart said, and all heads turned toward the TV.

"And now we'll take you to a festival that's not quite like any other festival you've ever been to," said the Channel Two reporter, her nose wrinkling a little as she added, "the Annual Guerneville Slugfest!"

As the camera panned over a crowd of people in a clearing in the redwoods, the reporter narrarated, "The little town of Guerneville is hidden away in redwoods so thick that the shade and moisture is perfect for the dampness-loving mollusk. So Guerneville residents decided to turn a problem into an asset, which they call the Slugfest." The TV showed pictures of children with balloons, and slug races, where the contestants were eye-to-eye with the participating slugs, cheering them forward as they oozed their way toward the finish line. Then they showed the cooking contest, where people were stirring pots and dipping chips, and there was Bart.

He was wearing a judge's badge on his lapel and sampling various dishes with the other judges, as the reporter stood by, narrarating. "Each of these dishes has to incorporate slugs, regardless of how many other ingredients are included," she said. The camera followed her as she walked along the display of entries. "Here we have Lemon Meringue Slug Pie, Crab and Slug Cheese Dip, Slugs in a Blanket," and she wrinkled her nose again, "and the winning entry, Slug Chili. Sound appealing?" she asked the viewers. "Well, remember, slugs have been a popular gourmet dish for some time, but then they're called . . . escargots!"

The camera cut to Bart then, and his name appeared on the screen. "Hey!" Bernie cheered, and even Claude seemed to have forgotten his troubles for the moment. Mark and I smiled at Bart at the end of the bar, and Rocco and Maria smiled at him, too.

"The Slug Chili was definitely the best," Bart said into the mic. "The flavor blended well with the other ingredients, and I was surprised with the subtle but pleasant aftertaste. The Crab and Slug Cheese Dip was a close second though," and he held a dip-filled chip up to the camera and then put it into his mouth. He nodded his head at the viewers and then smiled. "Very good," he said, and then chewed and noticeably swallowed.

The picture switched then and suddenly the sportscaster was reciting scores, and Bart's moment in the limelight was over.

"Good for you, Bart!" smiled Maria. Mark and Bernie and a few other customers raised their glasses to Bart and cheered.

Claude was quiet and seemed almost sober. "I don't know," he mumbled into his beer, scratching his chin and looking worried. "I don't know why a guy would eat those things."

20

You can't forget my love.
—Mark

When I came back after a week away in Oregon, Mark picked me up in Santa Rosa, where I'd taken a shuttle to from the San Francisco airport. I lit up when I saw him standing there through the shuttle bus window. We embraced, he picked up my bag, and we headed toward the parking lot and Betsy. I loved seeing my family, but I was glad to be home. Mark was happy I was back, too.

Mark had told me before I left that he was going to give me the final payment for Betsy, but I had told him to forget it. We had joint custody of Betsy. I was thinking while I was on the flight back to California about the times we'd shared, about how the late-night guitar concerts kept happening when we'd be alone at the end of the day, either in his cabin or mine.

As he played, we would take these musical journeys together, and it brought us closer together. I thought about how he'd play one song after another, all his own material, how many songs he had that I absolutely loved, how he would play and sing until he was finally happily exhausted, and we'd hold each other close in bed, listening to owls and occasional crickets as we dropped off to sleep. I was looking forward to more of that.

I was home. We parked Betsy and walked down the hill. It was getting dark, but the moon was out and the landscape had turned into a panorama of green-black hills with a soft white mist of fog drifting among them. Our feet knew the way. Even in the dim light, we knew where the ruts in the road were and where the rocks that jutted out from the grass on the side of the road were, and we avoided those spots without being able to see them clearly.

"Wow!" Mark exclaimed as the view spread out before us. "Only at this moment, from this spot, could this scene be experienced. This is what will be imprinted on our genes!"

It was breathtaking. These hills and canyons had become so familiar to me. Yet they were ever changing with the weather and the passing sun or moon. It was one of the most spectacular views I had ever seen. Even people we knew who traveled the world told us that nowhere was more beautiful than here.

"Some people never even imagine this," Mark said. "Just think of how filled some people's minds are with junk. This is magical."

As we continued walking in the stillness, the whoosh, whoosh of a bird in flight interrupted the silence. It flew right over our heads, and as it neared a branch of a tall tree, we saw its silhouette as it folded its wings to land. It hooted twice as it disappeared into the darkness of the heavy boughs of the tall tree.

When we got to my house, it felt so good to be there. I built a small fire in the woodstove and put on some water for tea. Mark rolled a joint, lit it, and handed it to me. He pulled his guitar out from under the bed, took it lovingly out of the case, settled onto the bed, and began to play.

Just because we haven't had the time we needed, girl,
you can't forget my love.
What I've given to you,
I give to no one else.
You can't forget my love.

In the morning light
I hope you see things my way, stay.
A million tomorrows may pass away.
You can't forget my love,
no, no way.
You can't forget my love.
oooh, ooh.
You can't forget my love.

Dear Mom,

It sure was nice seeing everybody, but it was good to get home, too. Thanks for everything. I had such a good time. The kids sure are growing up fast, aren't they? I guess that happens. I'm glad I got a chance to see them all. Your garden looked great, too. I guess we both know where I got my green thumb!

My flight was fine, and Mark was there when I got off the bus. He took me to dinner at the Blue Heron before we went home. It was almost dark when we got home. It's so beautiful here. I hope you can see it sometime.

We have some work planned in the garden, too. We planted some stuff before I left, but we want to get in another crop of beets and carrots, and get some zucchini and butternut squash in, too. These raised beds are really the way to go—really cuts back on the weeds. Bill tilled a section of the garden where a group of us are going to plant corn, about ten rows. We've had a big problem with gophers this year. The cats are supposed to be catching them.

I'll write more when I have more news. I love you so much! I'm glad you're doing so well and are staying so healthy. I'll try to call next time I'm in Occidental.
Love,
Joy
PS—Mark and I are just as much in love as ever!

21

> If I had to choose, I would rather have birds
> than airplanes.
> —Charles Lindbergh

Mark loved knowing about the local history of the area. From his friendships with the local fisherman, ranchers, and storekeepers, he heard stories of all kinds, but one of the best was the story of the Hole in the Head. Bodega Head was a small rounded hill that jutted out into the sea in Bodega Bay. It was a landmark in the town, and its beaches were popular. But the top of the hill was roped off with a No Trespassing sign. Mark wanted to show me.

We rumbled up the road in Betsy as Mark excitedly began the story. "It was the first, or at least one of the first, proposed nuclear plants in the country. It was around 1960, I think," he said. "But they stopped it. Those were some of the first seeds of the environmental movement.

There were all these protests. But PG&E dug this deep hole while they were trying to push through this nuclear power plant. That's what the hole in the head is."

As we drove along the winding coastal road, suddenly the ocean appeared on the horizon, and there was Bodega Head. We could see it as we rounded the last curve and came straight up to the coast highway. The sun was making the green grasses on it shimmer, and the Pacific Ocean that surrounded it, except for the one neck of land that connected it to the mainland, tossed silvery blue waves that sparkled and churned.

We crossed the highway and drove out onto the parking area by the beach. No one was around. Mark didn't hesitate to climb over the No Trespassing sign and head up a gradually rising trail. I hesitated. "It says No Trespassing," I said. "What if we get caught?" Mark looked at me like I was being totally illogical. "Well, you have to," he said, "if you wanna see it. Come on!"

We didn't have to go far. Even though there were a lot of tall shrubs, the dark water of the round pond lined with cattails was easy to see from that viewpoint. The water was dark, almost black, and the thick plants crowding around it added to the mystery. It looked really deep and a little treacherous. I didn't want to go too close.

Mark smiled, pleased with me that I had gone there. "Can you imagine this spot with a nuclear power plant on it?" He looked with disbelief at the thought. I couldn't imagine it with cone-shaped towers, fences, roads, and pillars of industrial steam. It was such a beautiful spot, a perfectly shaped green hill jutting out into the sea lined with sandy beaches, and this amazing hidden black pond at the very top.

"Aawwwkkk!" screamed a big blue heron, startling me by raising its big bony wings as it stood up out of a nest. "Awwwk!"

It shouted at me again. We were intruders. Probably the heron rarely saw any people up there. It wanted us to leave.

We walked back down the hill. No one saw us climb back over the fence with the No Trespassing sign and cross the small beach to where we had parked.

"So how come they didn't build it?" I asked as we walked.

"Oh, I didn't finish telling you," Mark said. "They hit an artesian spring, and the hole kept filling up with water. The fact that it was on an earthquake fault line—that didn't bother them. They were going to build it anyway. Can you believe that?!"

"Who owned the land back then?" I asked. "Didn't they try to stop it?"

"It was owned by Rose Gaffney, and she was against it. She tried to stop it. We should go to Bodega and talk to Ruth Burke. She knows all about it. She's kind of a local historian. Josh took me over there once and we saw all these news clippings she had collected, and she told us the whole story. Let's go over and see if she'll show us. You've got to hear the whole story, Joy!"

I had seen Rose Gaffney's tombstone once on one of our local tours and had heard her name mentioned. She was a local legend, crazy old Rose Gaffney, who chased some swimmers off her property with a pitchfork, talked to herself in court sometimes, and wore bright-colored mismatched socks with baggy dresses.

Ruth answered the door. She was glad to share her historical collection and invited us in. She had clipped every news story that had appeared over a fifteen-year period in five different newspapers. She also had copies of interoffice memos and personal notes to and from the local county supervisor, the PG&E agent, and Rose Gaffney. There were letters to the editor by the dozens, most of them not in favor of the plant, and the lyrics to a song by Pete Seeger, who had sung at a protest concert there. She wouldn't think of letting the eight heavy files out of the house but welcomed us to come back and read whenever we could. We did. It took three days.

Native Americans had been living on Bodega Head for thousands of years. The Miwok and Pomo tribes lived in relative peace and harmony with each other and with their environment. The head was rich with sea life. Clams, crabs, abalone, shrimp, lobster, mussels, salmon, and trout were found in the ocean and in the streams running to the sea.

For many years, Russian fur traders crossed the Pacific on trading missions, and in the 1840s the Mexican government, who "owned" the land as a territory, "gave" it to Captain Stephen Smith, who lived there with his Peruvian wife, Manuela. The captain died soon after, and Manuela remarried a guy named Curtis Tyler. By 1864, Bodega Head and the thirty-five thousand acres surrounding it was called Bodega Rancho, and Tyler sold the northern half to Miles Gaffney and the southern half to John Campbell. No one found out until much later that the old sea captain, Stephen Smith, still owned a thirteen-acre strip across the middle. The surveyors had made a mistake and the two parcels didn't quite join.

Through the years, the Gaffneys assumed that strip of land was theirs and used it for fishing, clamming, raising sheep and cows, and growing potatoes. The years passed, and eventually the land was inherited by Rose Gaffney, already middle-aged when her parents died and left her the property known as Bodega Head. Rose had grown up there, and after a lifetime of collecting and studying, she had one of the foremost collections of Native American artifacts in the area. She treasured those and mourned over the loss they represented.

An intelligent woman, sometimes given to periods of reclusiveness, Rose was aware of the value of the land. The green jewel of land had a value beyond money to Rose Gaffney. In 1955 the Department of Parks and Beaches wanted to buy the head, to preserve it as a public park. In 1956, the University of California wanted to buy it for a marine lab. Rose carefully considered both of these offers, wanting to find the best way to preserve the land. Suddenly, without explanation, both offers were withdrawn, and it soon became apparent why. PG&E wanted the land for its proposed project—the world's biggest nuclear power plant, estimated to cost sixty-one million dollars to build. The safety and security features of this particular plant were experimental and had never been used on an operating reactor. The plant would have a smokestack three hundred feet high and cables running across steel columns all the way to Petaluma to a substation. A deep hole would be dug to house the cooling tank of the reactor.

Rose refused to sell. She would never allow the land to be used for a nuclear power plant. The PG&E rep tried to wine and dine her, then to plead, then to demand, but Rose didn't give in. Even when she was told she might be forced to give up her land through condemnation procedures if it was determined that it was in the public interest, Rose still remained adamant. She would not sell her precious land to PG&E.

Condemnation proceedings began. PG&E started applying for permits and approvals through the Public Utilities Commission, the Atomic Energy Commission, and the County Board of Supervisors. At the time, PG&E insisted the plant might be steam or atomic. The company's actions, though, and the interoffice memos and public statements, made it clear that it was to be atomic and any opposition to the project would be repressed.

There was opposition right from the start, not only from Rose Gaffney. Locals and people from San Francisco united and formed a strong voice. Protests began, and hundreds of protesters marched while folk singers Pete Seeger and Mahalia Jackson led the crowd in singing protest songs. Journalists descended into the hole that had been dug to report on the fault line, the San Andreas Fault, which lies right on the site of the proposed plant, but still PG&E continued working, stating that the fault line wasn't active. The news media countered with the fact that it had moved sixteen hundred feet in the 1906 earthquake. PG&E insisted the fault line was of no consequence.

Finally, Mother Nature herself stopped the project. In digging the deep hole to house the cooling tower, PG&E struck an artesian well, a force of water so powerful it refused to be capped off, diverted, or pumped out. The proposal was abandoned. The hole filled with water, as it is now, surrounded by cattails, hidden from view, and overseen by a heron from its nest.

22

> Sometimes you never know the value of a moment until it becomes a memory.
> —Dr. Seuss

Mark encouraged my writing and drawing. He challenged me to find my own voice, to have confidence in my own work. Once I said, "I don't know if people will think my writing is good enough," and he said, "Then keep writing until you know for yourself that *you* like it, and that's what counts. Not pleasing someone else. Get to where it doesn't matter what someone else thinks."

It sounded like something he might have heard from his dad. His dad had influenced him to be original, to believe in himself, and to continue to hone his skills. The finest instrument won't reach its true potential without someone who really knows how to play it, he told me. When he was in high school, he told me, he would hole up in his room for hours, learning to play popular songs until, to the amazement of his friends, he could play them note for note without missing a beat. His dad would yell at him, "You're just mimicking!" His dad would say, "Write your own music!" He took those words to heart.

I was sitting in my cabin writing one afternoon when Mark came down the trail all excited. He told me he had heard that Moses was building a recording studio at Star Mountain. After writing so many songs at the ranch, Mark was thrilled that an avenue to record them was opening up right there. "It's been said that when you are ready for the next step in your journey, the way opens up," he said, smiling cryptically. "When the student is ready, the master appears." He had gone over to Star Mountain that morning to get the story. Star Mountain was the adjoining property on the other side of the West Canyon, where a similar community had sprung up some years after people began living at Wheeler's again. Moses owned that ridge, which was named Star Mountain after its starlike geographical shape from an aerial view. There were about eight cabins there and a main house at the top near the entrance. Now there would be a studio. Mark was thrilled.

It didn't take long to build. In no time, the completed studio stood ready and waiting, attracting musicians, mostly Mark and Cliff. They had great admiration for Moses, as he did for them. Mark told me about how Moses had gone to the South during the civil rights marches in the late sixties and recorded the sounds, the chants and singing, the speeches and the crowds and all. The recordings were in the Smithsonian as part of a special exhibit.

The studio was beautifully constructed and had a large room for the musicians, and a spacious control room with a big window facing into the playing room. The drum booth was a separate walled-off room with a window for the drummer to

see out. The main room had track lighting on the ceiling, thick carpet, and a woodstove. Moses had bought some recording consoles with two-inch tape like what the Beatles had first recorded on, a Teac reel-to-reel four-track deck with Dolby noise reduction. The control board was a Tascam eight channel. Mark had musical equipment, too, and he bought a synthesizer and speakers and mics. Cliff lived in a cabin right below the studio. He was one of the original Morningstar pioneers and was brilliant and creative. He and Mark spent many long hours recording their own originals and bringing in other musicians.

The studio did, as Moses had hoped, attract music and musicians. Cliff and Mark were there almost every day, often recording late into the night. Sometimes Cloud and Elm, who lived at Star Mountain, recorded too and brought in some congas and shakers. Local musicians, as well as some from the Bay Area, came too, but mostly it was Mark and Cliff creating and recording their own stuff. It was a dream come true. Both of them said in later years that the music they recorded together there was some of the best they had ever done.

One of my favorite songs, among many favorites, was like a symphony. Mark was experimenting with all kinds of sounds with his new synthesizer. He kept overdubbing layers, and the song developed into a mesmerizing orchestral piece. It started with a guitar part and then a timeless-sounding bell, like a gong, that rang and echoed as the music slowly built and the lyrics came in.

Walking very slowly,
almost on my way,
thinking 'bout the things I've done,
and it seems so very ever changing.
Where does one begin, it seems,
and we are strong
and our love it won't grow cold.

Walking very slowly,
almost on my way,
thinking 'bout those yesterdays.

The guitar lead climbed as the orchestra joined in with interplays of rhythms and melodies and harmonies, and a piano part on a journey, and then it all wound down together as if a conductor were bringing it back together into a slower pace,

and we are strong
and our love it won't grow cold.

23

Never let anything crush your spirit.
Because plenty of things in life will try to.
—Mark

Mark had a free spirit and a love of life that drew people to him. He was untamable and would never let himself be controlled by anyone else. It's what people loved about him and what drove them crazy. I accepted it. I admired it and wished more people had that unimpeded independence, that insistence on personal freedom. Plus he was almost always making music and making us laugh.

It seemed every rhythm and sound inspired him. In the sawing of wood, it was the back-and-forth rhythm of the bow saw. Walking, like when we'd be walking down the hill at night, he'd be tapping his finger on his leg, and then he'd start to hum or croon or channel lyrics that came to him, and a song would be born. He said it was like hearing a radio in his head.

Those nights we were at his cabin or mine, the woodstove would be radiating warmth and the windows would be open, and Mark would play his guitar and sing after dinner until we fell asleep. I marveled at my good fortune. Music spirits seemed to swirl around the house and drift in through the open windows, through Mark, through his fingers, and there I was carried away on the most mystical of journeys, traveling on a melody propelled by rhythm, closing my eyes and listening. I knew when I opened my eyes at the song's end, I had been somewhere.

It was one of those times that I first heard his song "Do I Wonder Why?" I loved the song right away and knew it would be one of my favorites for a long time to come. The reggae, island beat of it, the poetry of the lyrics, and the heart with which he sang it.

Does anybody really have a choice?
Are we hypnotized?
Does anybody make the same mistake
time after time?

The song floated out the open window and out into the world, and I had a vision of the song's future as he played. At first it was just me and him in a shack in the woods, and then the woodstove became a mixing board for recording, and the bed he sat on became a stage, the tall trees outside became a city skyline, and there were others in the room besides us. And then a wind came up that was like applause, and I could sense lots of other beings listening with me. It was no longer a private concert but a live performance before thousands at some point in the future, but somehow there now. Then I opened my eyes when the song ended, and we were again in the woods in a cabin, and the woodstove was a woodstove again. I sighed and said, "That was incredible." Mark looked at me and smiled. He knew what I meant, and then he said how grateful he was that the song had come to him.

The premonition came true when months later he recorded the song at Star Mountain. Years after that, we were at a popular club in southern California and I heard him perform the song again backed by a full band, and I remembered that night he had played it for me when we were alone in his cabin.

24

What seems to us as bitter trials,
are often blessings in disguise.
—Oscar Wilde

The winter sky cracked apart and the blue sky showed through the crack. Fog swirled around on its way somewhere else, and the sun reached through the holes in the fading clouds. Everything was wet and clean from last night's rain. The trees dripped with perfect round drops, and the steepest part of the trail slid wet mud with each step.

My jeans were still damp at the bottom from walking around late the previous night in the rain and mud. I was staying at Mark's house but had gone back up the hill and over to my house to get some things I needed. It wasn't cold enough to need a fire burning, so they never dried out. The mud had felt heavy and damp against my ankles, and I was glad to change into a dry pair of jeans and a dry shirt. They were the last clean ones I had. I added the damp jeans, mud and all, to the laundry bag.

Mark was in the dry spot of the overhang of the house, chopping some firewood for later. I started a small fire in the stove and whipped up some French toast for us, one of my specialties, with real butter and real maple syrup. I put some comfrey and yerba buena leaves in a pot of water for tea.

It was a good day to be going into town. We had our laundry in two bags to carry up to where we had parked Betsy. She was up at the top of the hill this time. With the road being so wet and muddy, we had decided not to drive down to the lower gate. I had a $50 check from my grandma, a late Christmas present, and I was expecting a tax return check from my waitress job last year. It was very part-time, and I only made about $3,000 a year. I had $224 coming back, and Mark had $60 he'd earned cutting wood for a neighbor.

Walking up the hill, each of us carrying a bag of laundry, we talked breathlessly about all that was going on, all the changes coming about in the community. We really had to push up the hill, but the fresh air forcing itself into our lungs felt good. Walking in was easy. It was all downhill. But walking out took some getting used to, especially carrying laundry on your back. Finally we got to the top. Betsy was a welcome sight. We threw our laundry bags in the back, and she started right up.

Bodega Bay had a laundromat. We threw our clothes in a washing machine and went to the cafe next door for some fish and chips. Mark could hardly wait to get to the studio. He had been going there almost every day, and most of the time I went, too. I loved seeing him and whatever other musicians were there doing what they did. Mark wanted to show me the new tracks he had recorded with a sax player from Guerneville. I had heard the guy play before, and he was fantastic. I couldn't wait to hear it. We would probably spend the rest of the day and night in the studio after we got the laundry done.

The last few months, some conflicts had been developing in the community. When Mark and I were at the studio, we felt comfortable and grateful, but when we came back to the ranch, things didn't feel the same. For a lot of different reasons, what had seemed like a family began to splinter, and each group was suspicious of others. We began to connect more with local people in the community than the people on the land. It wasn't the finest hour for many of us at that time.

Being at the studio, where Mark and Cliff were recording almost every day, was our getaway. In the studio, there was a positive creative atmosphere we all thrived on. Melo, whom we met when she moved to Star Mountain, had a strong, rich voice and had done some backup vocals for a local band. With her long red hair and her sense of humor and musical talent, she became a regular part of the studio. Mark and Cliff recruited Melo and me to sing backup vocal harmonies on some of their songs. It was so much fun. I didn't have the voice or range that Melo had, but most of the time I could hold my own. There were many times I hit an off note or missed the beat, but that could always be fixed in the mix. I just loved being a part of all of the music around me.

Ever since I had gotten a part-time waitress job in Bodega Bay just to make a few extra bucks, I had been bringing back pizza and beer to the studio, where Mark and Cliff would be recording into the night. I'll never forget those days. Music and laughter, creativity, all of us inspiring each other. We could play as late as we wanted. Not only was the studio soundproofed, but it was also somewhat isolated. Stepping out the heavy door, we would be under the stars, with a line of fir trees in the distance, the community garden across the gravel road in front of us, the main house with nobody in it, and the main road a ways off in the distance.

25

> There is a desire deep within the soul which drives man from the seen to the unseen, to philosophy, and to the divine.
> —Kahlil Gibran

I was in a thoughtful mood one day as I hiked up to Peter's Pond. It was on the adjoining property, but we were allowed to go there. Peter's was a community too, although a stricter and smaller, more organized community. The pond was an emerald green jewel surrounded by cattails with a single huge redwood standing at one end. The pond was as still as glass. I stood there in the June sunlight looking out to the horizon, then took off my clothes and jumped in. The cool water enveloped me. I felt buoyant and alive as the cold radiated deep into me, and then my own body heat warmed me from the inside out. I paddled around, smooth, easy strokes, and

swished my feet now and then, barely making a ripple. I felt like I never wanted to get out.

I swam until the coldness of the water had made its way into my bones, and then, slightly numb, I swam to the edge and climbed up onto the bank. The sun began to warm me immediately.

From this pond on the top of the hill, I could see down into the canyon and out toward the tall, distant trees on the horizon. It was a good place to sit and think. My heart felt so at home here. And yet, I was feeling some pulling at my heart. I didn't know what it was, but something else was calling. I felt that was the reason for the bad feelings in the community—sometimes life has to do something drastic to make you move, kick you in the seat of the pants until you move on. Even Mother Earth has to wean her children at some point. Take what you've learned and go out into the world, she was saying.

I was remembering the world I had left when I came to the ranch, a world where it seemed like the most important thing was to be actively acquiring things and aspiring to achieve status. How ironic that in the Age of Greed, as the eighties have been called, we were living a life of what we called voluntary simplicity. In the decade that gave birth to technology, we were living completely free of so-called modern conveniences and were instead going back to nature. In a rapidly expanding consumer society, we bought hardly anything. Our friends in the city were buying every new technological gadget on the market and running up their credit card debt to do so. We tried to live on as little money as possible and stay free of debt. We had so much more freedom and independence than our city-dwelling counterparts. There had to be some mysterious force of synchronicity playing out for our nature-driven lifestyle to manifest during that time.

We were aware of the differences in our lifestyle and considered ourselves fortunate to have not been swept up in that world. I knew so many people who were making their way through a system I wanted no part of. I probably seemed like a bum in some eyes. But being out here, I was never more sure of anything than that this was where my heart was. And yet, I was feeling this heartbreaking urge to think about maybe leaving. I loved it here but wasn't sure I should stay forever. I felt uneasy thinking the thought.

Mark was thinking about it, too. He hadn't said much, but his longtime buddy and bass player, Billy, had been hoping Mark would come back to Orange County. Mark had been on the phone with him quite a bit lately, and Billy always talked about the bands he was playing with and the musicians who Mark had known who were asking about him.

Once we started talking seriously about leaving, the sorrow set in. Just to think of tearing ourselves away from something that had become a part of us was somewhat of a shock. It would be hard to leave. The images we had in our minds of the land, we would always remember that, but to not live here, that was heavy on our minds. But to stay would be like never leaving home. You have to grow. Moving on is part of that. And the community was breaking apart. We weren't the only ones who were thinking of leaving.

By now, there was not even a question about whether Mark and I would stay together. He wasn't even considering moving south without me. We'd been together eight years, and while many people at the ranch still considered us an odd match, we knew how tight we were. Our love was deeply rooted and meant to last. We felt destined to have been brought together. We were soulmates.

We had more to do in our lives, and southern California was calling us. Mark had written and recorded so many songs.

It was time for the next step. I had no idea what to expect and felt eager to find out what lay ahead. When one door closes, another opens. We talked about it a lot, how hard it is to leave one place, but how exciting it can be to discover a new one.

26

New beginnings. Moving will be painful but necessary. What is ahead—changing of your life completely as you know it now.

I got the Tarot card reading from Melo's mom, who was a psychic. She held a silver bracelet I had been wearing for years. The main card was "New beginnings."

The first card of the future said, "Escape from danger."

The second card said, "Rising above obstacles and being victorious."

The third card said, "Happy family facing the future."

The fourth card said, "What is sure to happen—breaking away from the old way of life."

It was time for a change. No doubt about that. I had been wondering for a while, would this be my whole life? I loved the land, absolutely loved being there, and I had made a deeper connection than I thought possible. Mark felt the same. But just like we had been called to the ranch, now something else was calling us. We both felt it.

Mark had been wanting to be in L.A. again to get to the hub of the music scene. He was ready to plunge into the middle of it and take his music to the next level. That was where he grew up, and he still had a lot of friends and connections there. He wanted me to love it there, but he wasn't sure. He asked me if I would move to southern California.

It was no longer working where we were. We both knew that. But for all those years, we never imagined ourselves leaving. Perhaps we had learned what this place had to teach us. I was ready though, to see what southern California was like. So that was it. We talked it over and decided to go.

Mark's mom, in Huntington Beach, had a two-story three-bedroom apartment, and she always rented out the bedroom by the front door. It had its own bathroom and private entrance, and her current renter had just left. We could stay there while we looked for a place.

Loving the land the way we did made it hard to leave. But we knew that what we loved there would always be a part of us. Only the call of the next adventure would make it possible to say good-bye to this place. It was time. I kept saying it to convince my heart, in hopes something would turn us back and yet knowing it wouldn't. We kept moving forward with our plan.

We sold Betsy to a local young guy who would take care of her. She was too old to make the trip. We drove away in a used car we bought that we thought would work better for city life. Leaving Betsy and the coastal hills and a piece of our hearts behind, we headed for the open road leading south. Looking back at this land we loved and driving out for that last time, we were ready finally to move on.

We drove into L.A. at night, Mark at the wheel heading back to his home turf, and me, the stranger from another world, with my eyes glued to the masses of lights that spread out in all directions. For miles and miles, the lights of the cities dotted the night in what to me was incomprehensible human density, every sparkling light signaling people doing whatever they were doing, and it seemed endless and surreal. Mark was in familiar territory but had to keep his eyes and thoughts on the road. Sixteen lanes, I counted. Eight lanes going in each direction, multitudes of drivers whizzing by on one side and moving en masse with us on the other. We had talked about this, about how different it would be for me. Mark was hoping I would like it. I wanted to give it a try because it was the world he came from, and I loved him. So he drove on and on as I sat beside him spellbound.

When we left the ranch, where we had lived for eight years, actually ten for him, we couldn't have gone in a more opposite direction. On the ranch, we parked our cars and left them behind, hiking in the last half mile or so on a dirt path, to get home to our secluded cabin in the woods. In an average week there, I would see maybe six or seven people, and now this, this humanity out there in the darkness, hundreds of thousands, maybe millions, all living here in this place. My mind found it hard to grasp.

We were heading back to the birthplace of Mark's childhood dreams and dramas, where every several miles, memories of growing up here called to him as we passed. Back to the beaches and the wild Pacific Ocean that he loved with a passion. That ocean had made its way into his veins. It charged him up and humbled him all at once. Back to his old friends, his old bands and musician buddies, old girlfriends, his mother, sister, and all the unknowns that awaited us. We were excited, in different ways. For him it was a reunion, for me a new adventure. But it was new again to him, too. He didn't know what to expect. You can never really go back. You're different and so is everything else except for the land. The ocean, the beach, the wildness of the waves, all these are what they have always been. That's what makes it feel like home.

The palm trees, silhouetted along the shore when we reached Pacific Coast Highway, looked foreign and exotic to me. I had only lived in the Pacific Northwest, where there are no palm trees. To Mark, they were old friends, waving "Welcome Home." We drove along on the coast highway, just a two-lane highway finally, and the barely visible waves in the night roared and crashed onto the beaches as we cruised by, and the cars and people, even at night, were everywhere. The wave of humanity all around us, and me still speechless at the immensity of it all.

And then finally we were there. We parked the car that we had been in for some twelve hours or so and walked in to meet Mark's mom and see our new apartment. We had moved from a forest of trees to a forest of people, and I was intrigued. I could see Mark was relieved and hopeful that this part of our adventure, this long long drive, was completed. We didn't know what lay ahead, but we knew this was where we were supposed to be. I remember that moment right before we got out of the car. We looked at each other, smiled, and breathed a sigh of relief. It would be a big change. But it felt peaceful. It felt right.

27

I believe our love will last forever.
—Mark

Mark wrote this song a few years after we moved to Orange County. He'd been asked to write the lyrics for someone else's song, but they never ended up using this one. I loved it, though.

Broken hearts need not mean broken dreams.
I believe our love will last forever.
Though we go out on our separate ways,
in my mind, there will be time together now.

Seasons change and so do I.
Some are born and others die.
True lovers wonder why.
The mist clears only for a while
and hope can still be seen.

And then I think about the time,
a time when we'll be back together.
Broken hearts need not mean broken dreams.
I believe, I believe our love will last forever.

28

> Whatever you do may seem insignificant,
> but it is most important that you do it.
> —Mahatma Gandhi

On my sixtieth birthday, I dig through the closet in the guest room of my single-wide mobile home and carefully remove the turquoise binder from a box of stored mementos. This is the book I spent more than twenty years writing and editing, originally written by hand and then typed, this story I poured my heart into. Its vinyl cover and metal rings strain at its girth, almost three hundred pages with additional notes tucked into the pockets both front and back.

The turquoise binder has since lived in closets—years in my closet in our Long Beach, California, apartment, then in my closet in a small house in rural Scio, Oregon, and now in the closet of my guest room here in my hometown of Albany, Oregon. Yes, I went to high school in Albany, from where I ventured out on my path to explore the world, and now here I am, unexpectedly, back again. I went out in search of love and adventure, and found both. Twenty years the book has waited while I've wondered again and again—Is it finished? Is it everything I wanted it to say?

I thought the book was finished when I wrote that last page and gave it to three friends in succession to read and report back. That was in Long Beach. They all loved it and thought it was complete, but as my story went on past that last page and the years kept rolling by, I myself couldn't see it as complete. There was more to say.

As I sit on the guest bed now, the book feels heavy and awkward in my lap. When this story ended on page 289, Mark and I were living in Long Beach, in an inexpensive apartment in a multicultural neighborhood. He would often be sitting in the living room, guitar in hand, learning songs he would be playing at his next gig or writing new songs. I would be in the bedroom, writing, reviewing, typing.

The warm California sunshine would be streaming in through the second story windows, along with the sounds of neighbors closing doors, starting cars, calling out to each other. Street sweepers punctuated the summer air with their rhythmic droning. Green parrots that frequented the area on a precise daily schedule would perch on palm trees and telephone wires, screeching their arrival. The phone rings and Mark picks it up. It's his bass player. They're going over their playlist for the weekend's gigs.

Those were wonderful years in Long Beach and Huntington Beach. Mark had two bands of his own, playing his own original music, and played with numerous others, rock, blues, R&B, and just about anything that came up. He performed and recorded all over southern California, and toured Japan. Our voicemails were always full of offers and requests wanting him to play, and at one point he was playing five nights a week with three different bands. Mark said that he had played in all the best places in Hollywood and all the worst neighborhood dive bars. I loved seeing him onstage.

We had come from a quiet rural place and jumped right into the middle of this place of concentrated creative activity. It was two sides of the same planet. Because of the experience we had at Wheeler's living out in nature, we were drawn to find nature here, too. We had our favorite beaches, Crystal Cove and Bolsa Chica. We went hiking at Crystal Cove State Park, where there are hills and meadows dotted with tiny little springs and three-hundred-year-old oaks. You have to go off the trail to find them. Mark, of course, was always one to go off the trail and explore. We went for long walks on the beach, too, and talked about everything, from our years on the ranch to our present lives in southern California. But that was then.

Now it's very quiet where I am, in this over-fifty-five mobile home park where I live alone. Mark passed away more than fifteen years ago, and everything is different. Now he is a part of my life through memories, lasting bonds of love, stories we share about him, photo albums, and tapes and CDs of his music.

I no longer use a typewriter. Everyone has computers now, and cell phones. There's something about the book that needs to change with the times, too. I flip through the pages of the book I put so many hours into, so many years. But it's missing something. Now that he's gone, I want more than ever to keep his story, our story, alive. So this book doesn't end on page 289, and some pages I see are no longer pertinent to what I want to say. They needed to be written and to be recorded, but some of the pages are no longer necessary to tell the story. Now I know what I want to change about it, and why it hasn't seemed finished. It was a story about a certain kind of life. I want it to be about love, too. I had unexpectedly found true, lasting love on my journey. I hadn't planned that—as if anyone could.

That's what I learned after losing Mark and moving back to my hometown some thirty years after I left. That's what I learned turning sixty and looking back over time, as we tend to do at my age. That's what I learned by going back over the pages of the book that lived its entire life in the closet. Now I know the story I want to tell.

I took out a whole big chunk of the original book. The whole middle section was all self-righteous environmental diatribe when I was much more naive than I am now. I'm still an environmentalist—How can I not be? God made us stewards of the earth. But there's so much more awareness now and so many more potential solutions. A lot of what I had written felt redundant now, outdated.

I took out a lot of the personal bickering among friends, too. Communes are notorious for conflict. We like the idea of living together, but liking each other and getting along is sometimes a challenge. Everybody goes through some kind of personal conflicts in relationships at some point in their life. I decided that part wasn't unique or relevant enough to include. Out it goes.

What I left was all the meaningful, interesting, and important stuff. I think I finally got it right. I had found my book within a book. I wanted to tell about this incredible experience we had living on Open Land at Wheeler's Ranch. I wanted to tell about my life with my soulmate, Mark, and how blessed and fortunate we were to share our lives and our love. I wanted to put it all in perspective and have it make sense of where I am now.

In the community of musicians that we were such a part of in Long Beach, friends often commented to us that as a couple we seemed like we were just meant to be. Perfectly suited to each other and rock solid. That's how people remembered us. Losing somebody never really makes sense, but that bond of love gives you something to hold on to. I miss him so much. I think he would approve of this, my finally final version of my book. Sadly, Mark passed away in 2000 after a year in and out of the hospital. He was only forty-seven.

Bill Wheeler passed away, too. He died in 2018 at the age of seventy-seven. I saw a short interview with him on YouTube. I hadn't seen him in almost twenty years. He said that in declaring Wheeler's to be Open Land, he saw his actions as something bigger than himself. He was an amazing guy. We admired him. A lot of people were grateful for what he did.

I guarantee that anybody who spent any time there was touched by that experience, changed in some way that they carried with them from then on. It was an experience none of us will ever forget. And I find that the most important part about it is just that we did it. We lived on the ranch within this concept of Open Land. And it happened in a world where not too many people imagined that it could.

> Mark was the one who encouraged me
> to write my own music.
> —Pam Massey

*On the land, with our hands
we built a house that still stands
in our memory,
and you were lying next to me.*

*In the night, by candlelight,
everything was feeling right.
It was our destiny,
cause you and I were meant to be.*

*And you'd sing to the stars,
to the sound of your heart beating
through the strings of your guitar,
in perfect harmony
together you and me
we'd be singing to the stars.*

*From the redwoods, to the sands of Crystal Cove
and every step along the way,
watching from the stage, you'd see my smiling face
every time you'd sing and play*

*Now the years have passed us by
without a rhyme or reason why,
and it's a mystery
why anything in life should be.*

*And I know in my heart,
that you'll always be a part
of everything inside of me.
You'll always be a part of me.*

*And you'll sing to the stars,
to the sound of your heart beating
through the strings of your guitar,
In perfect harmony
together you and me
We'll be singing to the stars.*

—Music and lyrics written for Joy and Mark
  by Pam Massey

Acknowledgments

There are so many people to thank for their parts in the writing and publishing of this book. First of all, Mark, for sharing our lives, inspiring me, and always encouraging me to follow my dreams. I also want to thank my friends and family who encouraged me, inspired me, and supported me with their own memories that I was able to weave in—my sister, Pam, and Mark's sister, Christine, both of whom told me this is a good story, you should share this, and Dave, Cliff, and Billy, whose memories of Mark and their love for him added to my story, then and now. I want to thank my mom, Dottie, who set a great example for me in her own writing and publishing, and who inspired me to write even as a little girl.

    I want to thank Lill Ahrens for supporting my writing efforts and for pointing me in the right direction as I tried to corral my freestyle narrative into a cohesive composition. I was inspired by the other writing students in Lill's class, too—especially Dick Weinman, who published a beautiful memoir and with whom I shared mutual admiration and encouragement for each other's writing.

I want to thank Lorraine Anderson, who masterfully and beautifully edited the manuscript, helping me to perfect it without changing my voice, and Sheridan McCarthy, who helped me face my fear of publishing, my fear of relinquishing my anonymity and stepping out boldly to say, this is my story. Thank you.

www.ingramcontent.com/pod-product-compliance
Lightning Source LLC
Chambersburg PA
CBHW071400290426
44108CB00014B/1624